Eri[illegible],

I am wishing you all the best for your new start, sending lots of love & healing to your journey.

Have an amazing travel advanture & enjoy every minute

Veronika x

Diary *of a* Soul Reborn

A BREAST CANCER JOURNEY OF REBIRTH, SELF-DISCOVERY, AND DEEP TRANSFORMATION THAT WILL EMPOWER YOU TO DISCOVER YOUR TRUE SELF, RECLAIM YOUR POWER, AND THRIVE

Veronika Bubenickova

BALBOA.PRESS
A DIVISION OF HAY HOUSE

www.veronika-bubenickova.com
www.lotus-journey.com

Balboa Press books may be ordered through booksellers or by contacting:

Balboa Press
A Division of Hay House
1663 Liberty Drive
Bloomington, IN 47403
www.balboapress.co.uk
UK TFN: 0800 0148647 (Toll Free inside the UK)
UK Local: (02) 0369 56325 (+44 20 3695 6325 from outside the UK)

Print information available on the last page.

ISBN: 979-8-7652-1529-6 (sc)
ISBN: 979-8-7652-1528-9 (e)

Library of Congress Control Number: 2025912805

Balboa Press rev. date: 07/03/2025

"It is often in the darkest skies that we see the brightest stars."

RICHARD PAUL EVANS

Contents

Acknowledgments

First and foremost, I extend my deepest gratitude to my mum, my angel. Her unwavering support and love carried me through the darkest days. Despite not speaking English, she moved to England to live with me for nearly five months, looking after me, preparing fresh juices, and cooking for me when I wasn't feeling well. She was my best friend and companion throughout this journey, and her presence was a constant source of comfort. Her meticulous notes and journal entries, alongside mine, captured our shared experiences in unique ways.

To my dad, thank you for your unwavering mental support. Even though you couldn't be with me physically, your constant encouragement and belief in me were a source of immense strength.

To my brother and sister-in-law, thank you for being an integral part of my journey and providing amazing support throughout, despite facing your own challenges.

To my family in Slovakia, although far away, your love and support were always close to my heart. Your messages, calls, and unwavering belief in my recovery provided me with the courage to keep going.

To my cat Max, for being a constant source of comfort

and joy. His presence brought warmth and companionship during the toughest times.

To my dearest friend and business partner Klara, your guidance on a new diet, support with Max, and help during my operations were indispensable. Introducing me to healthy food and brands, and inspiring me to take big actions—whether it was a change in diet or starting a business—were transformative. Your fresh juices and thoughtful touches during my hospital stay were a lifeline. Your belief in me and my healing meant the world to me.

Sandra, your presence at major appointments and your help in organising the beginning of my journey were crucial. Your charity walk along the Norfolk coast provided much-needed solace.

Lisa, your dedication and support were invaluable. Running for me through mud and joining me for my first chemo session meant the world to me.

Ed, your support on the day of my diagnosis and beyond was a pillar of strength. Your emotional support and the lifts you provided were invaluable. Naming my energy "Vitamin V" gave me a source of inner power to draw upon when I felt depleted.

Becky, your little pressies brought joy with every chemo cycle. Martina and Gabca, your regular check-ins and support were a great comfort. Martina, your funny videos provided much-needed laughter, and thank you for running a race for me.

Shelley, thank you for guiding me on the right path with supplements and for your support during a difficult time for you as well. Your lifts to the hospital were greatly appreciated.

Ellie, thank you for always checking on me and supporting

me throughout. Melissa, thank you for always checking in with me, providing support, and giving me lifts.

And Klara R., for her introduction to spirituality and positive thinking in 2001, which has been a guiding light. A friend I haven't seen in years and who has no idea how much she influenced my whole life—and subsequently, even this whole journey.

To the Oncology, Breast Clinic, and Plastic Surgery teams at Addenbrooke's Hospital in Cambridge, and all the staff who provided incredible care during this time, thank you. Despite my belief that conventional medicine has much to learn from holistic approaches and techniques, your dedication and compassion made a profound difference in my journey.

And to the Silva Method instructors and the whole Silva family and community, thank you for all your support, for helping me to focus on healing rather than on the illness, and for believing in me and my healing.

Mel Ford, your introduction of Angelic Reiki into my life and your incredible teaching were transformative. Your spiritual healing session and coaching throughout my journey helped me uncover the emotional and spiritual root causes of the illness. It was like miracles were happening after these sessions. From a teacher and healer, you became a friend, and I am very grateful for that.

To my amazing homeopath Vicky, whom I discovered later in the process but who is still part of my life—thank you for being a deep source of comfort and contributing greatly to restoring my perfect health.

To everyone who walked this path with me, including my amazing neighbours—your love and support have been the foundation of my strength and transformation. This journey has shown me the depth of genuine care and the power of community. I am eternally grateful.

Finally, to the spiritual realm, I want to thank the Universe, Mother Meera and all the angels that helped me find my inner strength, guiding me to the right information, people, and treatments. And for the grace of God, that I found healing on my journey.

Disclaimer

The information provided in this book is for educational purposes only and is not intended to diagnose, treat, cure, or prevent any disease. It should not be interpreted as medical advice. This book is not intended to diagnose, treat, or cure your condition and is not a substitute for professional medical advice, diagnosis, or treatment.

The methods discussed in this memoir are intended to support health and healing, not to replace medical treatments. Whether you choose conventional or alternative treatments, or a combination of both, it is essential that you work closely with your healthcare professionals to diagnose, treat, and monitor your health situation.

Always consult your doctor or a qualified healthcare provider before making changes to your diet, fasting routines, supplement intake, or any other aspect of your health management, especially if you are undergoing cancer treatment or have other medical conditions.

The content of this memoir is based on personal experience, current knowledge, and research at the time of its creation. While efforts have been made to ensure its accuracy, I cannot guarantee that all information is complete, up-to-date, or applicable to every individual. The dietary and lifestyle suggestions offered may not be suitable for everyone, and individual results may vary.

By reading this memoir, you agree to take full responsibility for your health decisions and understand that the author and contributors are not liable for any adverse effects or outcomes that may arise from implementing the information provided.

Introduction

Welcome to a journey of an extraordinary transformation of an ordinary person and a story of profound healing on all levels – physical, mental, emotional, and spiritual.

This book is dedicated to all the incredible women who have been diagnosed with breast cancer, as well as their loved ones. It is a testament to the strength and courage that lies within each of us, and a reminder that you are not alone in this battle. You absolutely can do this!

This book is not about telling you what to do, but about empowering you to take control of your own journey, to seek the message in what the illness is trying to tell you, and to connect with your true self. And all you need is the power within you. That power has always been there. It just needs to be awakened.

This book is not just for those affected by breast cancer. It can be a healing catalyst and a source of hope for anyone who has been experiencing different health issues or has faced other life-altering events. It serves as inspiration that any trauma doesn't need to be the end of the journey, but the beginning of a transformation – if we are willing to change. There is always the possibility to see any life-altering event as an opportunity to grow or turn it into a purpose and a gift to others.

But of course, it is also for anyone interested in a story written by life itself. The story within these pages is not just about surviving breast cancer; it is about thriving, achieving phenomenal results, and experiencing a profoundly deep spiritual journey, healing moments, and personal transformation and growth.

For me, cancer was the biggest gift in my life. It taught me how to find joy and live, how to let go of stress. I found purpose and my life mission. Today, I help women affected by breast cancer to thrive, not just survive, both during and beyond breast cancer. And I am an advocate for breast cancer prevention, because I now believe that there is so much more we can do to minimise the risk of getting breast cancer in the first place.

I

My Life Before Cancer

I originally come from the Czech Republic. I was born during the communist era, when people had to hide who they were, conceal what they thought, and spirituality was suppressed. People could often lose more than just their credibility. So it comes as no surprise that the Czech Republic is frequently listed among the world's most secular nations. This had a tremendous impact on how I showed up in life. I come from a place where being spiritual is very judged. And although I don't follow any specific religion, I have been spiritual for a large part of my life but barely mentioned it to anyone because I didn't want to be judged. And this feeling didn't change even after I moved to England, with a much more diverse society where people respect other people's beliefs and opinions. It was deeply rooted in me.

I also grew up in the environment and times where it was normal to brush over emotions and be okay. I wouldn't even go out to see anyone when I felt bad. Most of my life, I pretended that I was okay even when I wasn't and was scared to show my emotions so that I didn't get rejected or ridiculed.

I had been someone who went along with things to keep others happy and to avoid conflicts. A big part of my life was identified with the hobbies and thoughts of the people surrounding me. It was as if I was with like-minded people, but it was just me adjusting to the environment. For most of my life, I lived the life of others to fit into society and did what was expected of me rather than being my true self and doing what I enjoyed. I got to the point that, apart from my job, I didn't even know what I enjoyed or had forgotten it somewhere along the way.

Most of my life, it was like I was living a double life – the public one that was the "accepted" way and the one more like me that very few (if any) people knew about. By doing this, I lost connection to what was important to me and to my soul, or maybe I never developed it, although I had some flashes of it from time to time.

I always felt like I had two completely different types of people within me. First, the quiet one, the thinker, the little writer or creator who wanted to be alone with its imagination or with the closest family because it felt emotionally safe. The other part was more wild and extroverted, living long in my imagination. It was who I wanted to become. The first time I awakened this part was during my younger age when experimenting with sorts of supportive substances.

Interestingly, after those experiences, I somehow knew that if I could be that part of myself in any chemically induced altered state, I could be like that without it too. But it was much harder to bring that part of me to life. I was learning it through work life, but in personal life, it was almost impossible to be the person I wanted to be.

I always loved animals. Growing up, I had a stronger

relationship to dogs, as apart from one of my neighbour friends who had a cat, most of the people in my life had dogs, so I classed myself more as a dog person than a cat person. I have had different animals as pets in life – hamsters, but also rabbits. Rabbits became part of the family and were both later, as cats, moving around freely around our flat. I even had a rat once, but only because I thought it was a little mouse when I got it. After a long time without a pet, I started to look after a friend's cat, Max, and it happened that he stayed with me and finally moved with me to the UK as well. This experience made me a cat person and a crazy cat lady.

If there was an animal that I felt always very connected to on a soul level, it is a dolphin—without ever even seeing one before. It was more of a spiritual connection. Interestingly, I built this type of soul connection to cats, especially to Max. But I feel like cats get attracted to me everywhere, like they feel the connection. There is also something spiritual and mystic about them.

Spirituality

My spiritual roots go back to when I was 18, just a couple of days after the attack on the World Trade Centre in New York. All I could hear was everyone talking about the tragedy and a potential start of the Third World War. My friend Klara R. came to visit me and told me that everything was fine and that whatever happens, happens for a reason. She introduced me to a life philosophy that explained why bad things can happen to good people. At that time, my spiritual journey began. I was thrilled to learn everything spiritual or esoteric. I started to study astrology, numerology, reincarnation, different forms of energy healing, and was obsessed with ancient Egypt. I spent hours choosing books in the library, reading them, and investing money in various courses. The first book I held in my hand back then was *You Can Heal Your Life* by Louise L. Hay. I would call it a discovery phase. I was going from course to course but never had enough confidence, dedication, or focus to practice any of it thoroughly.

I also went to see Mother Meera in Germany for a couple of darshans. Mother Meera is an Indian mystic who is considered by her followers to be an embodiment of the Divine Mother. She offers a blessing called *darshan*, which involves silently touching a person's head and looking into their eyes. During this process, Mother Meera reportedly "unties knots" in the person's subtle system and permeates them with light.

I also started following Sai Baba and his teachings. There are two prominent figures known as Sai Baba. Sai Baba of Shirdi was an Indian spiritual master who lived in the late 19th and early 20th centuries. Revered by both Hindus and Muslims, he taught the importance of self-realisation, love, forgiveness, charity, and devotion to God. He emphasised unity among different religions and performed many miracles, gaining a large following. Sathya Sai Baba, who claimed to be the reincarnation of Sai Baba of Shirdi, became a well-known spiritual leader in the 20th century. He was known for his teachings on love and service, as well as his reported miraculous abilities. He established numerous charitable institutions, including hospitals and schools.

I later had negative experiences with some of the Reiki healers and teachers, and that put me off. When I got a job in a bank and started to build a career in banking, life got in the way. I was enjoying a highly material-oriented life and spent much less time on the spiritual side. Although I still felt drawn to it, I wasn't settled enough to go much deeper into spiritual development at that time.

About 16 years later, and a few years after I moved to England, I found myself having a great job, finally in a long-term relationship, earning enough money to live comfortably—and yet there was still something missing in my life. When a spiritual shop opened in Ely, a place close to where I lived, I went there to have a look and saw a leaflet advertising an evening with Tarot. I had never been drawn to Tarot, so I asked the shop assistant if they also did Astrology evenings. He said no. Suddenly, I heard a woman's voice behind me saying, "My husband, Isaac, is an astrologer. I can put you in contact with him if you like." And this is how I met the first person to bring me closer to the spiritual world again. As it turned out, they lived just a 5-minute walk from my house.

A year or so later, Isaac dropped me a message that he would be doing a talk at a spiritual fair in Ely. When I looked at the programme, I decided to stay for the talk after his—about Angelic Reiki. My grandma loved angels—she had them everywhere. All her Christmas cards always pictured angels, and I was drawn to them. After my previous negative experience with Reiki healers and teachers, I trusted that with Angelic Reiki, nothing could go wrong because of the angels. And that is how I met Mel, who was giving the talk about Angelic Reiki. I booked a Reiki healing session with her, and when I came for my appointment, there it was—a picture of Sai Baba. I instantly knew this wasn't a coincidence. We connected, and in October 2020, I went on an Angelic Reiki healing course. Since that moment, my life started to transform exponentially. It was like blocks in my life started to shift and lift, and new avenues began to present themselves.

Shortly after the course, my partner and I had a crisis after around four years of being in a relationship, and I thought it was me who needed to change, so I decided to try counselling. The counselling opened up a big topic – communication issues. I started to open up and improve the communication between us, and for a couple of months, we both may have tried to do things differently. Everything seemed to work better for some time, especially in the period leading up to Christmas. We also started to look for a bigger house to move into, thinking it could solve our relationship problems. We thought maybe the house was too small for us, that we were on top of each other—not only the two of us, but also with his two boys staying with us most of the time, especially during lockdowns.

It was just a few months after the course when I woke up one morning—on the 1st of January 2021—and made a life-changing decision. I realised that I had lived in fear and doubt my whole life and decided to change that. I thought to myself: if I could be programmed for fear and doubt by the environment I grew up in and the experiences I had, I could reprogram my mind to whatever I wanted. I started with positive affirmations, bought myself a journal, and began working on myself. And things in my life continued to change.

A month or so later, I noticed a change in my right breast and could feel some lumps. I immediately started reprogramming my mind and listening to positive affirmations for many hours each day. I was referred to a breast clinic. Fortunately, they didn't find anything, and the conclusion was that because I had lost a lot of weight throughout 2020, some of the natural lumps in my breast became more prominent than when I had more fat in my breasts, and I hadn't been able to feel them before.

As I started to know and understand myself better, my partner and I eventually grew apart. I discovered new interests—my own interests—and my expectations and priorities in life changed. After a few sessions of counselling and trying to start again, the relationship eventually came to an end. It wasn't easy, as we were close, but it was the best decision for both of us to be happy. Looking back, the relationship couldn't last because after the counselling I began to transform—but for the relationship to work, both of us would have had to change. It became inevitable that we were no longer suited for each other.

Interestingly, when we were looking for a house together, there was such high demand for properties that we didn't even have a chance to get to a viewing most of the time. We searched for a house for months with no luck. As soon as we split up, I went to view maybe four or five houses, always got to a viewing, and I bought a house I absolutely love within two months. It was like the Universe was protecting me from getting a house with my partner at the time.

A few weeks later, I got promoted at work and was excited to take on a new challenge—to become a good leader and manager. It was also perfect timing to have a pay rise while buying a house. However, it wasn't exactly the amount I expected, but I was promised that my pay would gradually increase with future achievements, and I accepted it.

In autumn 2021, everything was amazing. I was enjoying being single again, had a job I loved, a manager and co-workers I enjoyed working with, and a new member of my team, Lisa, was just starting.

Then suddenly, my manager resigned, and I felt like our dream team was falling apart. Luckily, our closest colleague and my beloved friend Sandra was going to be promoted into the role, and I felt reassured that we could continue to work well together and keep growing and succeeding at what we did—despite the big loss of my manager leaving.

A few days later, something unexpected happened. It was just after the second COVID jab. My decision to have the COVID jab was one of the things I did only because of the pressure from society and to 'fit in' at work. But I never actually wanted the jab and tried to make a case based on my previous allergic reactions and intolerance to common medications like ibuprofen, penicillin, and a severe anaphylactic reaction to paracetamol that once landed me in A&E. I was worried about having another reaction and was hoping someone—well, the doctors—would stop me. But they said that the benefits outweighed the risks.

I always preferred natural remedies and felt very uneasy about the jab, but I went against my gut feeling. The only person who could have stopped me was me. But I was being "the good girl." I did it, but only from a place of fear—not to be judged. I knew deep within that I didn't want it.

Just about four days after the second jab, I drove to the office for work and planned to go to the airport after work to pick up my mum, who was arriving for my brother's wedding. But then, suddenly around lunchtime, I felt a very bad brain fog. I sat in a meeting and suddenly felt extremely unwell—something I had never experienced before. Then I passed out at work. I was shaking for a couple of hours and felt very ill. There were moments when I thought it was the end for me.

My colleagues called doctors, but no one asked me to

go to the hospital. No one has ever been able to explain what happened that day. It wasn't an allergic reaction, and it wasn't a known side effect. One thing is certain: if it had happened just a few hours later, while I was on my way to pick up my mum, I would most likely have crashed.

My manager drove me to the airport to pick up my mum and then took us home, as I was not able to drive. My colleagues brought my car home the next day. I was so fortunate to work with and for such kind human beings. It took me a few days before I could drive again and a couple of weeks to start feeling better.

During the breakup that year, I felt a strong longing for the company of someone who understood my culture and shared similar childhood experiences. Even more so because I was feeling homesick after all the travel restrictions during the pandemic. I told my mum that maybe I would reach out to a local Facebook community to see if someone from Czechia or Slovakia lived nearby. But then, with everything going on at work, my brother's wedding, and the purchase of a house, I sort of forgot about it.

On 9th December 2021, I was finally moving into my new home. It was the busiest time ever for me—I felt quite stressed and quickly went to the post office to send a parcel.

A woman stood in the queue in front of me. When it was her turn, I overheard her saying to the service assistant, "Could I post these letters to the Czech Republic and those to Slovakia?" I immediately wanted to speak to her. But it was my turn next, and I thought she would be gone by the time I posted my parcel. To my surprise, she was still there. I felt shy but asked her at the end where she was from, and she said—from the Czech Republic! I told her I was Czech too, and she suggested we meet for coffee.

And that was how I met Klara, who became my beloved friend, an unwavering support in life, and a source of inspiration when it comes to investing, sustainability, and a healthy lifestyle. We both wanted more from life and looked for ways to get out of the rat race—something we talked about a lot at the beginning.

Since January 2022, I started having problems with my periods, and finally, in May 2022, the doctors ran tests and found that my iron levels were very close to zero.

They prescribed me iron tablets, but I had an allergic reaction to all the iron tablets and liquids they gave me. I had to cancel my holiday to Portugal as I ended up in A&E and wasn't able to board the plane. It took several weeks until I finally received an iron infusion and started to feel better again.

In one of the incidents during the time I was being given iron tablets, I had to call an ambulance but wasn't able to open the door for them. Luckily, I was able to wake up my friend Klara in the middle of the night, and she came to my house to open the door for the ambulance. That was the second moment in my life when I thought it might be my last day. When the ambulance arrived, they didn't see a reason to take me to the hospital, as it was severe anaemia, and I started to feel better after a few hours. It was probably a sudden and significant drop in my oxygen level.

But it was during this time, when my iron levels and haemoglobin were so low, that I could no longer continue living my life at the same pace as before. I was forced to slow down, which was very challenging for me. I am a very active person—I was running around 8km every day, working hard and more hours than I was contracted for. I was constantly thinking about side hustles in my spare time, exploring ideas on how to create another income stream. My pace had been too fast.

I was overwhelmed by all the opportunities for building a side hustle that could eventually replace my 9-to-5 job. I kept jumping from one thing to another, never resting, never allowing myself to have fun. I lived my life like everything had to be done and completed before I could enjoy myself. I didn't appreciate that everything in life is a process. During the time I was experiencing low iron levels and was forced to stop running and walking, I had to rest.

It was at that time that I first heard about the Silva Method. This method teaches how to control your own mind and access altered states of consciousness in order to improve your life. I had such a strong feeling about it and started reading a book.

Based on the book, I began practicing how to go to the alpha level of mind—a different state of consciousness (frequency) where we can use visualisation and imagination to manifest things in our lives, solve problems, and enhance our intuition. I was fascinated by it and wanted to learn more. I had an inner feeling that this was right for me. And unlike in the past, when I jumped from one course to another, I knew that this and Angelic Reiki were the two things I wanted to pursue and master. I even felt that maybe becoming an instructor of such an incredible method could be an avenue to explore.

The book mentioned an intensive four-day course, which I wanted to sign up for immediately. I discovered, however, that the course I wanted to attend clashed with my rescheduled holiday in October.

I was so eager to learn that I purchased online access to some lessons and exercises so I could make a start until I found a suitable course date. Eventually, I managed to book the course for December 2022.

In the meantime, I went through a series of investigations to determine why my iron levels had dropped so suddenly—but nothing was found. The preliminary conclusion was that the body was so low in iron that it had started to prevent itself from losing any more blood and that was why my periods stopped temporarily.

Just before the doctors discovered that my iron levels were low, my work life fell apart. Sandra resigned, and I became the last of the three people in our smaller team. I thought about applying for her role, but after understanding the reasons why both previous managers had left, I was convinced I would end up in a similar position before long.

At the same time, with Sandra's help, I set off on a different path and wanted to progress my career within product development. I envisioned going from the Lead Product Owner role—managing a small number of people—to a Head of Product role, and eventually striving for Product Director and Chief Product Officer positions. In other words, stepping onto the career ladder toward an executive role.

But I also faced the uncertainty of having a new manager and not knowing whether we would work well together. Still, I had a clear development plan and was fully dedicated to making it all work.

We identified that in order to achieve my goals, I needed to work on my leadership and public speaking skills. I also felt the need to master public speaking because someone had made comments about my communication and accent previously.

I signed up for a public speaking course and joined Toastmasters International, a nonprofit organisation that helps individuals improve their public speaking and leadership skills through structured meetings and supportive peer evaluations.

But with Sandra leaving, I initially thought I could still make it work. However, the workplace changed into an environment where I didn't feel understood or supported enough, and I found it hard to stay inspired. I also felt under immense pressure and was doing the job of multiple people, trying to fit it all in.

I liked doing my job well, so looking back, I realise that I put a lot of pressure on myself too.

II

Events Leading Up to the Day D

Shortly after my new manager started, I went on holiday to Malta and fell in love with the place. I went for a run along the beach every morning, did my morning routine, and was ready for an adventure with my friend Klara by 9 AM. This made me think that if I lived there, I could simply be happy—in the sunshine, by the sea, where my soul feels at peace—and I could still be at work by 9, full of joy.

I remember sitting on a bench, watching and listening to the sea, and crying because I didn't feel valued, supported, or understood. I felt so unhappy and didn't want to come back home. It wasn't just the usual feeling of not wanting to return from holiday—it felt like I was leaving a place where my soul was truly at peace.

I even put a note in my calendar: wait for bonus in June, resign, and move to Malta. I checked everything—what I would need, how I would move my cat there. And when I thought about what I would do there, I imagined finding a job and also creating retreats for busy people.

After my return, things at work got worse. Now it wasn't just me feeling demotivated—it was the whole team. I felt like I was hitting a brick wall. I lost my spark, and I knew the only solution was to find another job. I'd had that feeling for a while and had attended some interviews in the autumn, but nothing came out of them. I was looking for a more senior role, so I knew it would take time.

Then, after one meeting at work, I ended up feeling absolutely demotivated. I felt unappreciated and unsupported—especially on an emotional level—after sacrificing so much of my time and effort, working many hours of overtime to make things work, and carrying so much on my shoulders. I had a complete meltdown, and instead of my usual 27-mile drive home, I ended up driving over 100 miles. I couldn't stop crying or driving.

I had never felt so uninspired at work in my whole life. Demotivated. Disappointed. Resentful. There was also grief—grief after losing the best two managers and colleagues I had ever worked with. And I knew that was the last straw. Although I didn't want to leave the company, didn't want to leave my amazing co-workers, and didn't want to leave the new manager who seemed very nice and supportive—I felt like there was only so much he could do. And maybe it was me who needed a change.

I didn't feel like my role and desire for career development was understood. And career progression was very important to me—I couldn't accept being held back.

So, I found myself overworked, overstressed, and unhappy. I knew I had to leave to save myself and my sanity. I felt like I was in a broken marriage.

Reaching a new career milestone

The very same week after this incident, I was invited for an interview for a Head of Product role with a different employer.

That weekend, I had the first part of the Silva Method basic course. It was held over two weekends, and it was phenomenal. I was so excited to learn and put into practice some of the most amazing mind self-control techniques. By using the techniques from the course, I felt like I did so well in the interview—I felt calm and confident.

The week after, I advanced to the second round. On the Friday, just before my second-round interview, I had another disappointing meeting at work where I felt unsupported and misunderstood. I went into the interview determined to get the job. During the interview, I felt like my potential future manager and I were on the same page, that we viewed things in a similar way, and I had a strong sense we would work well together. But of course, you never know who you're up against.

I enjoyed experimenting with more Silva techniques to program for a successful outcome.

The following Tuesday, I received a phone call with a job offer—and a salary offer that exceeded the maximum advertised—exactly what I had asked for. I felt relieved and so excited to move on to this new opportunity. I knew I could do it because it came to me naturally, and it was exactly what I wanted to do.

I also knew I wanted to use the higher salary to save up for deposits so I could invest in properties. I was so serious about it that I asked for an exemption in the employment contract to be able to participate in a property business.

Klara and I had been talking about opportunities to create

passive income and secure our retirement, with the goal of at least semi-retiring early. We were already studying a course about setting up and running a limited company, so it was already in the plan. I felt like I had unlocked a completely new potential, and a new life of success was starting to reveal itself.

It was the best Christmas present I received that year—I signed the contract on 23rd December 2022, and I agreed to start on 27th March 2023.

I felt like I was on top of the world and was simply looking forward to the festive period and a well-deserved break.

I also felt like I could finally start living and enjoying life more. I planned for my Czech friends to visit in February, I started going to the theatre more often, I planned a Royal Ascot race day in June, and a celebration of my 40th birthday in Ibiza in May. I felt alive.

At the same time, there were still some challenges I wanted to overcome.

A vicious circle of overeating and overexercising

On the physical level, I had a severe addiction to sugar, I was overexercising, and I didn't like my big belly. I was slim most of my life, but there were times when I was quite chubby. And when I gained weight, it was most visible on my tummy. I had people congratulate me because they thought I was pregnant. The truth is that I have never been happy with my body, especially my tummy.

I lost a lot of weight when I moved to England because I started eating regularly and going to the gym at least five times per week. After losing over 10 kilograms, the tummy got smaller but was still sticking out. I didn't adhere to the routine all the time, and my weight fluctuated. I started walking extensively during lockdown and later added running. At first, it was a replacement for my commute. I was drawn to exploring the countryside, and I found a new hobby and a way to recharge energy after a stressful day at work. I was losing weight at the same time and managed to reduce the tummy fat to some extent. But then I found myself in a state where I didn't want to lose any more weight elsewhere—just the belly fat. And I wasn't able to make it happen, even with excessive exercising. So one of the goals I wrote down in my journal was to lose tummy fat in 2023 because it was knocking down my self-confidence.

I have generally been a very addictive person. One of the most challenging habits I managed to get rid of in my life was smoking. But it is quite common that we exchange one bad habit for another one. I replaced it with vaping, and that proved to be an even worse habit than smoking. I learnt to vape everywhere, and it became so bad that it started to bother me. I couldn't imagine travelling anywhere by plane, and I was dreading every journey with my ex-partner's kids, even if it was just a 10-minute journey. These were the moments when I found the habit unbearable. It limited my life, and one day I just ended it. It was more challenging than quitting smoking.

Then I became addicted to sweets. I would go through one or two bags of sweets every day. When my gums suddenly got much worse, I transitioned from sweets to biscuits, chocolate, and cakes. Then I suddenly found myself in a vicious circle of excessive exercise and overeating on sugary food. I used to tackle stress or strong emotions in the same way as smoking and vaping. Instead of having the occasional piece of cake in celebration of something, I would have cake, biscuits, and chocolate in excessive amounts every day. And when I went out, I would have more than one cake to celebrate.

All I cared about was my weight and maintaining it—because I was happy with my body weight, just not with the shape. I cared little about health. I knew that I wanted to do something about it, but the addiction was stronger than me.

Deep resentment

On an emotional level, I felt some deep resentment and was unable to forgive. I felt like I was unable to forgive this person for what they did and how they acted, and that they didn't even have the courtesy to apologise or at least try to make things better.

I suddenly felt like I was in such a toxic environment that I was dreading every day of serving my notice. But I still worked hard to hand everything over properly because there were many other co-workers that I valued and respected, and I cared about them being okay after my departure.

I knew from my lifelong interest in spiritual subjects and the psychosomatic causes of illnesses that deep resentment can manifest in the body in harmful ways. But it was too raw to emotionally move forward at that time.

Questioning my beliefs

On the mental level I was overplanning and overthinking and my logical mind would override and question anything that wasn't backed up by science. After I completed the Silva Method course in December and had some great successes with some of the techniques. But there was something on the back of my mind questioning everything and seeking a logical explanation. That had an impact on my faith. I wrote in my journal in January 2023 that I wished to strengthen my belief in the power of my mind.

My life vision & dreams

During the Christmas break, I took the time to reflect and to create my life vision. And I knew I wanted to do something to help others, to help animals, to help the planet. I wanted to inspire others. I wanted to become an inspiring leader, and I wanted to learn how to speak publicly for the very same reasons. I wanted to write a book and other digital content, and I wanted to teach others about well-being and positive thinking. But I knew little about it all or just didn't know exactly what to share. It was a little of everything I knew, and I wasn't sure that was enough.

I wanted to have properties abroad and achieve financial freedom and travel. That's because I wanted to retire or semi-retire by age 45—eventually leave the 9–5 job. And I wanted the high-paid job to save up for deposits to buy properties and fund the beginning of the business set-up. I also wanted to have my own brand one day—with natural perfumes, home décor, and so on. I also got to the point of being ready to meet a partner, a life-long companion who I can share all this with.

There were also things like being able to inspire and help those who need it. I had a few images of dolphins as well, as I always felt deeply drawn to them.

I was playing with the idea of moving to Malta or spending half of the year there and running some retreats for corporate clients, busy businesspeople, or people who were burnt out. These were dreams—I didn't have a clue how I could get there from where I was. Although it felt like the year 2023 may not have been the right time, as I was just about to start a new job, I put my Malta move on hold—but still kept it in my vision.

Questioning life purpose

The first time in my life I knew roughly what I wanted to achieve long term and what I expected from life. Something meaningful. But still I questioned my life's purpose. I wanted to do something that would fulfil me and that would give me a purpose. I signed up for a Life Mission course which is available only to graduates of the Silva Method in January and I was hoping for it to help me to identify what is it that I should do in my life.

And when the year 2023 started

In January, everything was working out perfectly. I had regular meetings with my future manager, and we were planning my onboarding to the new company where I was meant to start on the 27th of March. He was a very inspiring person, and you could tell from the way he acted that he was a great leader—supporting a healthy environment where people feel motivated, inspired, supported, developed, and understood. I was organising handovers at work and had some leave, which enabled me to have a 10-day break between the two jobs. I planned to go to Slovakia to see my family and to meet my dad after four years. We hadn't seen each other for that long because of the COVID pandemic and my dad not being ready to travel—or for me to travel—for some time.

There was still one last investigation I had to undergo to understand why my iron levels had dropped so much and so suddenly, as they hadn't found anything else. This was a colonoscopy and gastroscopy scheduled for the 29th of January. It was just to ensure there was nothing in my intestines preventing iron from being absorbed properly. And I said, "I hope this will be the last hospital appointment and I can just relax and move on in life." I visualised a good outcome and believed it was just a good MOT of my body.

So I believed that I was in the best part of my life. I felt like I was on top of the world. I was very successful in my career, moving to a more senior role in what I thought was my dream job, with a significant salary uplift that could enable me to save a substantial amount of money every month. I wanted to invest it in a property business that we planned to set up with my friend Klara. We had started a course on how to set up and run a limited company and were about to begin a more advanced property course specialised in the area we were interested in.

The vision I had was to do a high-paid job, save money to start a side hustle, and create some passive income so I could semi-retire and have the time and money to create something that would have true meaning and make a difference in the world.

But then, suddenly, the unexpected happened.

And then, something unexpected happened

On Friday, 20th January, after work and a relaxing bath, I noticed my right breast felt hard, lumpy, and slightly swollen. A lump near the nipple unsettled me, but with GP offices closed for the weekend, I had to wait until Monday. Though anxious, I tried to focus on the weekend.

Saturday brought a long-overdue chat with Czech friends, and we planned a visit for February. On Sunday, 22nd January, I attended a Life Mission course in London. It revealed that my purpose was to lead, guide, and teach—but I had fears to overcome: fear of judgment, of being hurt, of worst-case scenarios. One intuitive message stuck with me: "The right info comes when you need it."

On Monday, 23rd January, I saw a doctor. They fast-tracked me to a one-stop clinic, saying it was routine for any breast lump. I wasn't too alarmed—two years earlier, a lump had turned out benign, and this one appeared just before my period, which the doctor said might explain it. I even wondered if I had injured myself.

Instead of doom-scrolling about cancer, I focused on breast health. I learned about the lymphatic system and how dairy, sugar, and caffeine can block it. I began cutting sugar from tea, intermittent fasting, and redoing the Silva Method course to strengthen my mental resilience.

By Wednesday, 25th January, I journaled that the breast looked different. The next day, I started visualising and mind-programming for healing.

On Friday, 27th, I had a powerful massage and crystal healing session, where the healer sensed a female spiritual guide—possibly Mother Meera, whom I'd been connecting with. It felt like a protective presence, especially as I was nervous about my upcoming sedated procedures.

On Sunday, 29th January, I had a gastroscopy and colonoscopy. Everything went well. My digestive system looked healthy, though two biopsies were taken to check for gluten intolerance. I wasn't too concerned—any issue would just mean a diet change.

My period ended, and the breast didn't change. Moreover, on Saturday, 4th February, I noticed another lump, the size of a grape, appearing on the top part of my right breast. I could not only feel it but also see it, as it was sticking out. I could also feel a little pain or discomfort. The evening before, I had a glass of wine and thought that the breast issue had worsened after the alcohol. But from that point on, I was getting more and more worried.

I tried to mind-programme for a good outcome, but my expectations, feelings, and beliefs weren't aligned with what I was visualising.

On Sunday, 5th February, someone who had no idea what I was going through sent me a speech from Anita Moorjani, who had a near-death experience through cancer. It resonated so deeply with me that I started to get worried there was a reason this video had found its way to me. I tried to work on the deep resentment I felt and on forgiveness, as I already believed these emotions can be linked to cancer on an emotional and spiritual level.

I tried to visualise a good outcome for the appointment on the 6th, did affirmations and meditations, but it was like something in the back of my mind already knew.

It felt different from when I went through this process of finding changes in my breast and waiting for the appointment at the breast clinic two years earlier. I even said to my friend Klara, "If it's bad news, I will change my diet completely." It was like I was expecting it. Looking back, I didn't want to admit it or accept it, but I just knew. I couldn't get myself to believe it would be a good outcome.

Later in the evening, the night before my appointment at the breast clinic, I called my mum, crying. I was so scared. The fear was paralysing. My mum tried to say things to make me feel better, but it just pushed my buttons because it sounded like she wasn't worried at all. So I hung up.

I cuddled my cat Max, who was the biggest source of comfort, put on some guided meditations, and they helped me to fall asleep and get at least a good night's sleep.

III

Day D - Diagnosis

My appointment in the one-stop shop clinic was on 6th February at 8:50 a.m. at Addenbrooke's Hospital in Cambridge. My plan was to visit my friend Ed afterwards, and we agreed that I would call him when I was finished to see if I still had time to pop in for a cup of coffee.

It was 8:30 in the morning when I messaged my friend about the breast getting worse over the past few days. I tried to see it as a good sign rather than a bad one—because if it were serious, it wouldn't change so rapidly. But as I sat there, I focused on leaving the clinic with everything sorted that same day. In truth, I felt huge fear.

Everyone around me—my family, friends—were just trying to comfort me with words like, "It won't be anything serious," or "They'll give you some tablets, and it'll be okay," and similar. But when I looked at my right breast and the way it looked, the shape just reminded me of something nasty or evil. I can't explain in words the emotion that the shape of the breast brought to me.

It was 8:50 and they were slightly delayed. First, I went

to see a specialist nurse. She asked me some questions and looked at my breasts. She said she couldn't promise that I would be all sorted the same day, but that they would definitely have some answers.

They sent me for a mammogram first, and then I waited for an ultrasound.

The room was cold and dark. I got undressed, and the nurse offered me a blanket. I was shivering—it was a combination of cold and fear all together. Everything just happened so quickly. The radiologist came in and started preparing everything for the ultrasound. He told me he was going to put gel on my body and that it would be cold. I said, "Do whatever you like, just tell me good news." He didn't say anything to that.

Once he performed the ultrasound, he said they would like to do some biopsies. That meant using something like a large needle with a hook at the end to take tissue samples to be sent to the lab. As he was explaining what he was about to do, I said many times, "Do whatever you need to do, as long as it's good news." Every time I said this, he didn't react—he stayed quiet and carried on with the biopsies.

It was so painful. The nurse was holding my hand, talking to me, trying to distract me. I was crying. I was scared, cold, and felt lonely and desperate. They also inserted clips into my breast to mark the area. They did three biopsies. On one hand, it felt like a lifetime; on the other, everything happened so fast, and it felt like so much was going on at once.

One of my friends, who had recently gone through the one-stop shop clinic, told me she waited a week for her biopsy results. So when they finished and told me to get dressed and come to another room to make an appointment for next week, I wasn't surprised. I felt physically drained after the examination, and my mind wasn't in the right place either. I got dressed and wanted to work on my positive mindset and mind programming until the next week so that I would receive good news.

The nurse asked me if I wanted a hot chocolate, and I said yes—I needed something tasty and warm. My expectation was that I'd be given the hot chocolate, make an appointment, and off I'd go, with one more week to wait for the results from the lab.

The nurse took me to a different room. When the door opened, I entered a much nicer room than the rest of the clinic—there were armchairs with nice pink cushions, and it was decorated very warmly.

I sat down and started drinking my hot chocolate. It was almost 11 o'clock. The specialist nurse and the radiologist came in and sat down. They spoke very calmly and quietly and said they had some bad news—I had breast cancer.

I suddenly felt like I left my body, like I was just observing all of this. It felt like I was only dreaming. It was like time stopped and everything froze.

They said it was likely to be curable, but they wouldn't know for sure until they did further imaging.

My next appointment at the breast clinic was scheduled for Thursday, 16th February, which was the day my two friends from the Czech Republic were coming to visit me for a few days. When I mentioned it to the nurse, she recommended bringing them with me to the hospital and not postponing the appointment.

I asked what the chance was that it wasn't cancer, since they still didn't have the results of the biopsies. They said that from what they had seen, it was 99% likely to be cancer.

They also advised me not to stop doing anything and to carry on with everything as normal. My concern was about exercising, and they said the more I exercised, the better.

They asked if I had someone to go to, and I said that I had planned to visit a friend. They suggested that would be best.

Looking back, there were so many signs during that appointment—everything was clear all along. During the physical examination, when the nurse said, "We will definitely have some answers for you today," she must have already suspected something from what she saw with her own eyes. Then when the radiologist didn't react to my repeated "as long as it is good news" comments, and later when they offered me the hot chocolate and brought me to the beautiful room in the clinic—it was obvious.

When they left the room, I didn't know what to do. The first person I called was Ed, because I had been planning to visit him on the way home—if time allowed—so I could go back to work. But suddenly, I had no sense of time, and work was the last thing on my mind.

I broke the news to him, and we agreed that I would go straight to him. I left the hospital around 11:15, but I was so unable to process anything that the drive took me nearly 45 minutes instead of 15. I kept missing turns, trying to call a few of the most important people (using my hands-free set). I couldn't process it. I was in complete shock and also felt angry with everyone who had told me it wouldn't be anything serious. I felt like they had underestimated the situation, and I wasn't even thinking straight.

I got to Ed's, and it felt much better not to be alone in my own head (although I was anyway). He gave me so much support. First, he called our manager and told him what had happened and that I wasn't in a state to come back to work. We both got the afternoon off and went for a walk. Ed tried to talk about things, and I tried to concentrate on what he was saying, but it was like my brain was just trying to analyse and process everything that had happened that morning. I zoned out many times during that walk.

When we got back, we chatted for some time, and Ed made me a sandwich because I hadn't eaten in 24 hours. After spending a good three or four hours with Ed, I decided to say goodbye and go home. Klara wanted to pop by to see me, and I was planning to visit my brother later that evening as well.

And it was as I was going back to my car, reaching for the handle, that something suddenly changed. It was like my mind—which had been like a computer processing billions of data points at once—finally found a result. Everything unfroze. Something clicked. I turned around, looked at Ed, who was still standing in front of the house ready to wave at me as I left, and I said,

"I've got this. I will heal. I don't know how, but I will."

Between the day D and final diagnosis

And from this very moment, I was at the beginning of a mission. On the way home, I called my two friends and told them the news, and said that I would pick them up at the airport on Thursday, 16th—but the first place I would take them to would be Cambridge Hospital. They were both shocked but very supportive, and I assured them that we would have a great time together no matter what.

By the time I got home, I had a complete mess in my mind—I didn't know what to do first. But I knew the first steps I was going to take to get my health back. I decided to eliminate all processed food, refined sugar, meat, and dairy products from my diet. At first, this was to clean my lymphatic system.

In the past, I had heard of people who healed cancer by juicing. So, the second part of my battle plan was to get a juicer and start juicing.

Last but not least, I believed that every illness has a root cause on the emotional and mental level. I knew I had some forgiveness to work through and that I needed to learn how to love myself more.

When my friend Klara came to see me, I asked her for help and guidance. She was my inspiration when it came to healthy eating, and she even helped me look at new juicers online. However, when I mentioned my battle plan to my friend Sandra, she said she had a juicer she barely used at home and that I could have it.

I also somehow felt that this had a higher purpose and deeper meaning in my life. Maybe there was a reason why this happened to me. It was just after I had questioned my life purpose and created my life vision board. I believed this was not the end—it was just a part of my journey and the beginning of a new life.

All I did that afternoon and evening was talk to people, so by the time I got to bed, I was exhausted. And I managed to sleep well.

On Tuesday, 7th February, I set off to work, as I was working in the office that day. I think I still wasn't familiar with my new diet and what I could and couldn't eat, so all I ate was a homemade sandwich, and then I had only fruit and nuts for the rest of the day.

I drove to Sandra's after work to pick up the juicer and stayed for a cup of tea. This was my first day without refined sugar—and it went surprisingly well. The combination of bananas and nuts helped me greatly. What had been a huge problem and addiction suddenly disappeared, as if I had waved a magic wand.

When I came home, I joined a Silva Method graduate group, and the Silva community and family have been the greatest support since. I joined the group and raised a question about how to program for good outcomes when you've just been diagnosed with breast cancer. The instructor helped me with some mental exercises for mental clearing and for creating an image of loving myself to perfect health. Everyone attending was also very supportive. I was also added to a healing group that I attended most Fridays during my journey.

On Wednesday 8th February, I started with juicing. I drunk fresh juice 3 times per day, only had lunch and some healthy snacks in the afternoon and did intermittent fasting 19:5 (which means 19 hours fasting and 5 hours of eating window) so that the body has the chance to start detoxify. I was told to carry on with my life as normal so I attended a Toastmaster meeting in the evening and delivered a practice speech. I practiced a lot but felt like compared to the speech I delivered back in January it wasn't how I wanted as my mind was still going off thinking about the diagnosis. And at that stage I didn't want to share with anyone there.

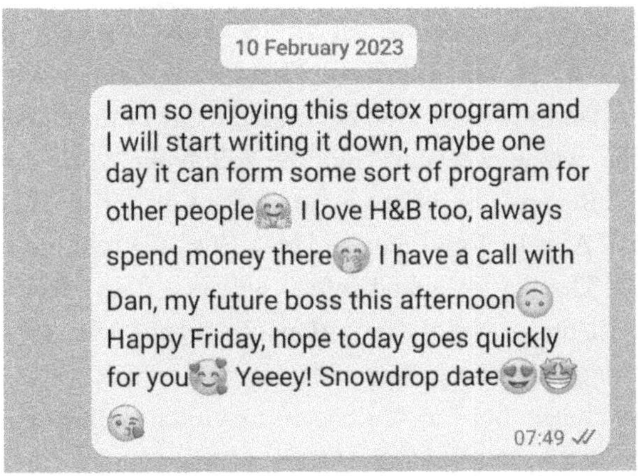

On Friday evening, 10th February, I was about to go to bed and read when I started to feel very unwell. It felt similar to the episodes I had when my iron levels and haemoglobin had dropped so much.

The next morning, I was driving to meet my friend Sandra for a walk at one of the National Trust places, and I really didn't feel myself. My head was spinning, and I was getting worried. We walked and then had lunch there, and that was probably when I had a little bit of refined sugar in the sandwich at the café—my first since the radical change to my diet. I felt better immediately after the sandwich, so it seems like the small amount of sugar in it satisfied my body enough to feel normal again without further sugar top-ups.

After lunch, I felt well again and the symptoms never returned. It must have been a reaction to the withdrawal of refined sugar from my diet. But at the time, I wasn't sure what it was, so I asked for a haematology appointment to be brought forward to check my iron levels again. This was just a regular check-up I had been having following the iron infusions. I was booked for a blood test on 16th February and then a consultation on 20th February. This meant that was another clinic I had to take my friends to on the day of their arrival.

The whole weekend and the following week I spent researching and also booked two sessions of spiritual healing with my Angelic Reiki teacher, Mel. She also told me about Gerson Therapy. I looked into it and just didn't feel like I could risk opting out of conventional treatment. I wanted to do something alongside it. And with Gerson Therapy, you need to make a choice. But I took some of the guidance from Gerson and applied it to my juicing. Hence, my morning juice became apple and carrot every day. I also reduced celery and cucumber from my diet, as they have a high amount of sodium, and I ate a lot of bananas, as they are high in potassium.

Gerson Therapy is based on research suggesting that sodium feeds tumours, while potassium helps shrink them. I was also visualising positive outcomes from the hospital every day. Yet, I was still very scared.

Although I was in my notice period, my manager

approached me to speak to a dedicated department at work to seek any support and help they could offer—even during my notice. I asked for full-time home working, and that was granted. I agreed to explore counselling and scheduled an appointment, which I subsequently cancelled. I couldn't imagine having any more appointments and decided to opt out of counselling.

Although counselling had helped me in the past with other issues, I felt like it didn't go deep enough for me this time. I didn't want to just dig into the past and leave it open. I chose spiritual healing, which used less logic to dig into the past and more energy healing to clear it—with some big *aha* moments. I also felt that being part of the Silva community was the best support I needed.

I had a fantastic Silva family supporting me and encouraging me to think positively from the start. We had a WhatsApp group where people would drop requests for distant healing, and I asked for healing into the results of my scans—so that they would come back the best they could, and that the cancer wouldn't be incurable. I accidentally spelled "incurable" as "imcurable." The reactions I got were amazing—people saying that the Universe didn't want me to spell it correctly or even think about that word. And they helped point me and my mind in the right direction.

Being around like-minded, positive people played a bigger role for me than counselling.

Having graduated from the Silva Method just before it happened, I felt like I had the best "equipment" to control my mind and use it to create a better outcome for my life. I also felt like all of this happened for a reason—and that finally, after I had defined my life vision, after I had learned about controlling my own mind, after I had achieved some sort of success and a well-paid job, after I had manifested all of this—this couldn't be it.

But the truth was, I didn't know. I didn't know if it all worked. And I didn't know that I would be sitting here now, writing this book.

The reason why I didn't want to prioritise counselling wasn't because I was rejecting help or suppressing my true emotions. I knew how scared I was—I just felt like I needed something to lift me up and bring my energy up, rather than focus on and amplify what I already felt.

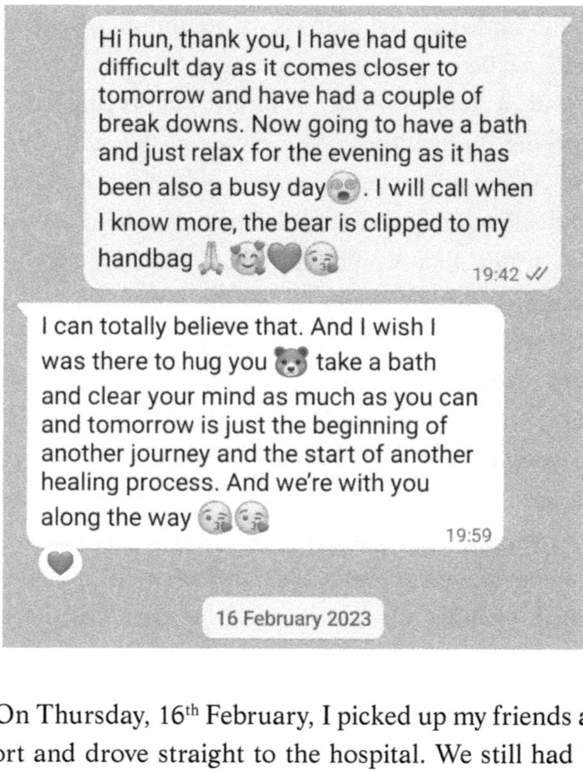

On Thursday, 16th February, I picked up my friends at the airport and drove straight to the hospital. We still had time, so we had a coffee, and I remember introducing them to my latest favourite drink—chai latte with coconut milk. Although it had some refined sugar in it, this was the only challenge when eating out. So when I ate out, I would have to sacrifice the refined sugar rule, as it was almost impossible to avoid. On special occasions, I would allow myself a chai latte with coconut milk.

We were meeting my brother, who was joining me for the appointment. I really wanted to see the specialist nurse who had given me the initial diagnosis. There was something so comforting in her voice and eyes. And it was her—it was very comforting to have her there, as I just felt a great connection to her. She invited us into the room together with the breast surgeon.

They presented me with the results of the biopsies. Two of them were from two tumours—one behind the nipple, grade 3, and another above the nipple, grade 2. The third biopsy was a sample of a lymph node, and there was no trace of cancer found. I was diagnosed with HER2-positive breast cancer.

They outlined a treatment plan consisting of chemotherapy, mastectomy of the right breast, and potentially radiotherapy. But there was hope that I would be cured—and that was a relief. They gave me an A5 folder with information about the different treatments and space for notes.

But they continued with the next steps, and said that over the following week I would be very busy with different appointments. One of them was a CT scan to show whether the cancer had spread. They also wanted to do two more biopsies of other lymph nodes on the same day to check if the cancer had spread there, as the lymph nodes appeared enlarged. If it had spread to the lymph nodes, it would change the treatment plan. If it had spread further, it would be incurable. So, no relief after all—and another week of uncertainty.

Luckily, I had a few days with my friends visiting, and it was going to be a busy week until the results of the additional biopsies and CT scan were back, and until the multidisciplinary team could review them and either confirm or adjust the proposed treatment plan.

I was also told that chemotherapy would move me into menopause, and I was advised to consider visiting a fertility clinic regarding preserving eggs. This was to be discussed with the oncologist.

One of my questions was: would I be able to start my new job during chemotherapy? And because it was a remote job, sitting at a desk, they said I should be able to. They also encouraged me to carry on as normal as much as I could, and to stay active.

It was interesting that, despite both of them wearing face masks, I could still feel the connection with the specialist nurse. It was like her eyes were talking to me, telling me everything would be okay. Every time the surgeon said something, I looked at her, and it was like I found hope and reassurance in her eyes. I was so scared that I remember squeezing my brother's hand throughout the whole appointment.

When we finished, I went for the biopsies of the lymph nodes. When I got back into the waiting room where my friends were waiting, I was feeling quite positive and tried to look at things rationally. I knew there were three options: it was "just" breast cancer, or it had spread to the lymph nodes and they would need to adjust the treatment plan, or it had spread further and was incurable.

No matter what, I just wanted to enjoy the time with my

friends. I didn't even think about a potential "death sentence" at that moment, and in the back of my mind, I was dedicated to trying anything to heal—no matter what the results were. That said, it did play on my mind during the quiet times. But luckily, there weren't many quiet times in the week to come.

After leaving the clinic and saying goodbye to my brother, I took my friends for a lovely Thai lunch near my home in Ely. Later, we visited a private clinic so I could get my iron and haemoglobin levels checked. It had been a long, emotionally charged day, so we went home to relax.

That evening, we celebrated—my new style. We clinked glasses filled with fresh juice served in elegant gin glasses. It felt good to share this with friends who understood the significance of these small rituals. My phone didn't stop ringing—people were checking in, offering support, and sharing uplifting stories. One, in particular, stood out: someone who had recovered from terminal cancer using just a few drops of CBD oil daily. Stories like that gave me real hope.

Then I received a phone call I hadn't expected—from the partner of Isaac, an astrologer I knew. I assumed she was calling to reconnect after the holidays, but instead, she told me that Isaac had passed away from cancer. I had believed he was in remission. As it turned out, the doctors had only scanned him from the neck down and missed tumours in his brain. He had beaten cancer twice before, but this time, he felt his journey was complete.

She shared some of the remarkable things Isaac had done during his healing journeys and offered me the supplements he had used. I've continued taking those same two supplements ever since. She also recommended a Chinese herbalist. The timing of her call felt uncanny—like Isaac's soul had passed the baton to help me now, much like I believe my grandmother's spirit watches over me. It was the start of a series of "coincidences" that made me feel deeply supported by something greater. I began saying to people that maybe there was a reason this was happening—maybe I was meant to help others one day.

Having my friends around during this time couldn't have been more perfect. None of us knew what would unfold when we planned their trip, but it felt divinely timed. We hadn't seen each other in four years, but we picked up like no time had passed. We had a beautiful time together—one day in London and another in Cambridge. As we talked about life, I found myself sharing my dreams and everything on my vision board. I had so much I wanted to accomplish, and for the first time, I truly felt—it wasn't my time to go. I had a mission here. After learning how to use my mind to create a better life, it was like the Universe kept nudging me with signs that everything would be okay.

As I rambled through my dreams—writing, healing, helping others—my friends laughed and said, "You'll need many lives to achieve all this!"

On Sunday, 19th February, I dropped them off at the airport and headed straight to my CT scan. That afternoon, I had a spiritual healing session with Mel. It turned out to be one of the most powerful yet. Although we were in different places, the energy between us was palpable—like a solid column of resistance that refused to move.

Later, we focused on diving into limiting beliefs and past emotional wounds—especially around not feeling good enough or worthy of love and healing. The energy was intense, but it felt like another piece of the puzzle clicking into place.

My affirmations that came out of it were:

- *I am worthy*
- *I accept myself*
- *I am important, I count*
- *I deserve to be healed*
- *I am unconditionally loved no matter what I have or haven't done in life.*

We often feel like we should be punished or that we don't deserve something, simply because there's likely a childhood pattern of being rejected, punished, or denied something—either when we did something we shouldn't have or, on the contrary, when we didn't do what we should have.

I also had an aha moment when I truly understood the saying, "Everything is about perspective." A few weeks earlier, receiving a breast cancer diagnosis felt like the moment my life fell apart. At this stage, the "breast cancer only" diagnosis was a piece of cake compared to the other options. And this is a citation of the exact words from my journal!

On Monday, 20th February, a new team member was joining. With me leaving on 17th March, the plan was for her to take over the tactical and day-to-day parts of my job, while my manager would take on the strategic part and line management responsibilities. I felt so bad for her, joining at such a difficult time. I had told her about my resignation earlier, and I had an extensive handover plan—everything was perfectly scheduled. But now I had to share my news, and it was likely that I wouldn't be around at all until 17th March.

Still, her first day went well. We had a nice lunch, and then I was on my way to the haematologist to discuss the dizziness

I had experienced a few weeks earlier and to check how I was doing in terms of iron and haemoglobin levels.

It was a private clinic, and you can really experience a completely different level of service. My haematologist was shocked when I shared my diagnosis, and he was trying to be very supportive. Looking at the blood test results, he said my levels were all very good, and he suggested that he could discharge me from his care, as I would be under extensive care through the NHS during my cancer journey.

He was interested to hear about my case, and I shared how scared I was, waiting for further results and hoping it was "just" breast cancer. It was all quite nerve-wracking. He sympathised and said he would have a quick look to see if the results from the CT scan and lymph node biopsies were back. However, he explained that I would still need to wait for the consultant to explain what it meant for me after the multidisciplinary meeting at the hospital.

But then—he saw that the reports had been filed just a few minutes before we started our conversation. There was one letter stating that the CT scan didn't show any further spread and that the biopsies found the lymph nodes were inflammatory but non-cancerous.

Wow! This felt like another sign from the Universe telling me I was fully supported.

I didn't expect to know anything before Thursday, 23rd February, when I had an appointment scheduled with the oncologist. I didn't want to get too excited, but it sounded very reassuring!

On Tuesday, 21st February, I had a strange experience when I went for a run. I often get into a zone while running—receiving good ideas, emotional clearings, or solutions that come to mind. I also visualise a lot when I run, and have inner aha moments, especially when running in nature and quiet places.

That day, I felt as though my spiritual guides, Mother Meera and Sai Baba, were holding my hand. I could feel from the bottom of my heart that I wanted to heal, that I wanted to love myself unconditionally. I cried the entire way—and then cried more at home. It felt like a huge emotional clearing, with a deep, powerful outcome: "I want to heal."

It was extraordinary. I felt as if the cancer diagnosis had helped create a stronger spiritual connection. I felt so close to the Divine and to God.

Later, I went for an MRI scan, which I had been worried about because they were injecting dye into my veins—and I've always been anxious about unknown substances entering my body after previous adverse reactions. But they gave me an emergency button, so I felt quite safe in case I felt unwell. It was my first MRI scan, and I was surprised by how noisy the machine was!

On Wednesday, 22nd February, I went to the Chinese herbalist in Cambridge and also had acupuncture to balance the energies in my body. She prepared a mixture of herbs for me to take home. I was taking it twice a day, mixing it with cooled, reboiled water.

Sandra was coming with me to my first oncology appointment on 23rd February and had started preparing some questions, which was so kind of her—it was much-needed support.

Since attending the Silva Method graduate group on the 7th and then the 14th of February, I had been following my instructor's advice and was visualising 2–3 times per day for good outcomes from my CT scan and biopsies. The great thing about the Silva Method is that once you start practicing it, "coincidences" begin to happen in your life.

For example, the fact that I thought I was low in iron again when I had the reaction to refined sugar withdrawal—and that I brought my appointment with the haematologist forward, and he happened to look into my record. Interestingly, the results of my biopsies and CT scan were uploaded just a few minutes before he checked. And although he couldn't give me the final diagnosis, the things he read from the report sounded rather promising.

These "coincidences" are a fantastic form of feedback for what you are mentally working on.

Final diagnosis

Thursday, 23rd February, was a big day. I remember driving to the hospital to meet my very good friend Sandra, who had offered to come with me to my first appointment with an oncologist. As I was driving on the motorway, listening to music and thinking about good outcomes, the phone rang. It was the specialist nurse from the breast clinic—the one I felt deeply connected to.

She called to tell me that I would receive the full diagnosis and treatment plan from the oncologist, but she wanted me to know personally that the cancer hadn't spread anywhere and that all the lymph node biopsies were clear. What a kind woman she was! I felt incredibly grateful—and burst into tears. I cried during the call, and I'm crying again as I write this.

I managed to call my closest loved ones before arriving at the hospital.

There was a lot of traffic, and both Sandra and I arrived very close to the appointment time. We met at the car park and then walked through long hospital corridors to reach the oncology department. It wasn't easy to find—it felt more like a maze than a hospital. We passed a few people along the way, but once we entered the Oncology department, it was packed. So many people sitting, nurses rushing around—it was the busiest department I had ever seen.

Because it was my first time there and I wasn't sure what to do, that kept my mind busy. I had to go to the reception, then they sent me to get my weight and height measured, and then we waited in the waiting area for quite a while. Eventually, I was called in.

Sandra and I entered the consultation room, and the oncologist invited us to sit down, advising me to record the conversation as there would be a lot to take in.

She reviewed all the scan results. There were some minor findings in my intestines and pelvis—nothing serious, but a follow-up CT was recommended in six months to monitor for changes.

Then came the topic of fertility. She explained that my periods might return after treatment unless hormonal therapy was needed, but there were no guarantees. I'd already been told about the option of a fertility clinic referral, though that process could take weeks. Given the speed at which the cancer was spreading—nearing the lymph nodes—I decided to go ahead with a Zoladex injection on the spot. It temporarily shuts down the ovaries by blocking oestrogen, and since I wasn't strongly focused on having children at the time, I accepted it without hesitation.

We also discussed hair loss. I was referred for a wig fitting and told about the cold cap, which can sometimes reduce hair thinning. I agreed to give it a try.

She said we should see visible changes in my breast after two or three chemo cycles—roughly 6 to 9 weeks. But her tone suggested she believed the cancer had already spread to my lymph nodes. I reminded her the biopsy results showed no cancer in the nodes—just inflammation. She looked at me and said, "Oh, I don't believe that." Wow. That kind of comment could have shaken me—but thankfully, I'd been working on my mindset.

After the hour-long consultation, I met with the specialist nurses who support breast cancer patients. I was given a "red card" (Rapid Response Card) that must be shown in emergencies—chemotherapy weakens the immune system, and oncology patients require specialised care.

I also met the research nurse, who asked if I'd be willing to take part in a study. I agreed—it felt like the right thing to do. She asked about doing another biopsy. I told her, "I'm not happy, but I'll do it," and we both laughed. The paperwork let me choose how to participate. I agreed to everything except one thing: I didn't want my tumour implanted into mice. Even if it was for science, I couldn't bear the thought of another living being suffering like that.

By the end of our conversation, it turned out they needed two or three biopsies, not one. I joked that she should go into sales—she made it sound like one! Despite that surprise, I still agreed.

When we left, both Sandra and I cried. The emotional

weight of the day—and seeing how many others were going through the same battle—was overwhelming.

With a confirmed diagnosis and treatment plan in place, it was time to have open conversations with both my current and future employers. I needed to explore whether I could stay in my current role a bit longer and wait to start a new job until my treatment was completed, or I could start the new job while still undergoing treatment.

My official treatment plan

My official treatment plan consisted of seven chemotherapy treatments. The first four chemotherapy treatments were Docetaxel and Phesgo. Phesgo is a targeted therapy for HER2-positive breast cancer, which is also used as after-treatment. It is a combination of drugs Herceptin (trastuzumab) and Perjeta (pertuzumab).

They planned a mastectomy of my right breast 4–6 weeks after finishing the last chemotherapy. This usually includes removing lymph nodes that have, or could have, been reached by the cancer. It was explained to me that biopsies provide a good indication of whether the cancer has spread, but the most accurate result can only be determined by removing the lymph nodes during surgery and examining them in the laboratory.

They also outlined some after-treatments such as radiotherapy and continuing the targeted therapy trastuzumab. But they asked me not to look that far ahead, as it all depends on how well the body responds to the chemotherapy and whether the lymph nodes removed during surgery come back clear or cancerous.

I have always been an advocate of herbal and natural

remedies and don't like taking any conventional pills. I am also allergic to some—for example, paracetamol, penicillin, or tablets used to treat iron deficiency. When I fall ill, I don't take any pills unless necessary and prescribed by a doctor.

Therefore, being told that I needed chemotherapy was very hard for me. I didn't want to do that to my body and had very mixed feelings about it all.

But I didn't want to play with fire. I wasn't far from the cancer starting to spread to other parts of my body. My belief system wasn't strong enough to opt out of conventional treatment, and I felt like I could work with my mind and body to tackle the side effects of any conventional treatments.

I decided to proceed, combining conventional and complementary treatments.

Problems are nothing but wake-up calls for creativity.

GERHARD GSCHWANTNER

My approach to healing

Although I didn't have a plan for my whole healing journey to start with, I decided to make significant changes to my diet from the next day after they first told me and introduced some supplements and complementary treatments immediately.

The first few days after the diagnosis, I had only blueberries and apples for breakfast, then a panini with goat cheese, bananas, grapes, and unsalted nuts. The days after were very similar. I added juices to my diet and ate different lunches, for example, sweet potatoes with mushrooms, courgettes, and goat cheese. I found a tasty, healthy pre-made korma sauce that I just mixed with vegetables. I was trying to transition from being a cheese lover by replacing it with a different cheese not made from cow's milk—later eliminating it too.

Before I was told I had cancer, I believed I was eating healthy food—apart from my addiction to sugary treats, mainly chocolates, cakes, and biscuits. I kind of disregarded that. I didn't realise how much harm I was causing to my body. Because it wasn't about the weight. I ran every day, so you would never say that I ate an excessive amount of sugary food. But I was eating so many vegetables and fruits, and low-fat dairy products, and considered my diet to be relatively healthy.

I had already been in a process of realisation some time before the diagnosis. I wanted to get rid of the sugary snacking habit, but it was stronger than me. I had already managed to reduce the amount of processed food I was eating.

I grew up in an environment where meat was the main part of the diet—especially processed meat such as sausages, salamis, and pâtés—combined with dairy products like cheese, cheese spreads, sour cream, mayonnaise, dressings. And all that combined with lots of bread, dumplings, potato pancakes, or potatoes baked in too much oil. I grew up on processed food in combination with sugary treats.

Yet I wanted to make radical changes to my diet but wasn't sure what I could actually eat. I knew I wanted to detox the body as much as I could. I didn't know what or how to do it—but I had this inner feeling. It was like something was guiding me.

I didn't feel like I was sacrificing something—but rather starting a new way of loving my body more. I wanted it to be part of my identity. I did it from a place of love for myself, to fuel my body with good quality and healthy food.

I ordered new cookbooks and started experimenting.

I studied a lot about supplements to support a healthy diet and to help me detox, recover, and relieve side effects faster. I discovered how most mainstream supplements are synthetic and filled with additives. So I made sure I always chose organic and natural supplements—mostly in the form of powder from a plant or mushroom—that I could mix into my fresh juices.

"Eat your food as your medicine, otherwise you will have to eat medicine as your food."

STEVE JOBS

I love running and walking, and I continued to run 5–8 km almost daily. Movement helped me release tension, process emotions, and stay grounded.

At the same time, I worked on mastering my mind every single day. The number one rule I followed was simple but powerful: focus on healing, not the illness.

That mindset required open and honest conversations with my parents. I told them I would do whatever it took to heal—even if that meant doing things differently than they would. I asked for their full support with no judgment or unsolicited advice. I said, "If I decide to heal by standing on my head all day, I don't want to hear 'you should' or 'you shouldn't.' I want to hear, 'Great, do it—whatever helps.'" And to their credit, they really did support me fully. They cheered me on and backed every decision I made, which meant so much.

One of the first challenges I encountered was the reaction from people around me—especially when I changed my diet. Some of the closest people in my life didn't understand. They questioned what I was eating or avoiding, and made comments like, "That's not good for you," or "You need to eat this instead." I knew they meant well, and were acting out of love and concern. But it reminded me of how unaware I once was too.

Still, I had a deep inner knowing that I was on the right path. This approach had already helped so many survivors, and I trusted that if I stayed consistent, my results would eventually speak for themselves. I followed my gut feeling and stood by my choices, even when it wasn't easy.

This is also why I chose not to join any cancer support groups. I didn't want to surround myself with stories of illness, fear, or victimhood. Instead, I joined the Silva Method community. I attended meetings for Silva graduates and those exploring the method, and there I met women with or recovering from breast cancer who were just like me—focused on healing, not the illness. We had different techniques, but shared the same powerful mindset. That kind of energy is contagious—and healing.

I also joined a Friday Zoom healing group where a small group of us would meet and send healing to each other and to others. Being part of this circle of positivity helped me stay emotionally strong and spiritually connected.

I then felt called to find a "safe space"—a place that brought me joy, calm, and inspiration. I found it on one of my walks, near a field that gave me a feeling of peace and strength. In my mind, I turned it into a symbolic power station. I imagined the field filled with solar panels, absorbing sunlight and storing energy for me—a healing grid. That became my personal energy reserve.

During one of my runs, I gave this place even more meaning. I started visualising it as a national-grid-style hub where I stored my inner strength—what my friend Ed later named Vitamin V. Ed and I had worked together, and because my name was long, people at work just called me "V." After my diagnosis, Ed was amazed by how calm and strong I was. He said, "That's your superpower—Vitamin V." The name stuck.

So that field became the home of my Vitamin V—a mental image I could return to any time I needed strength, energy, or encouragement. Every time I walked or ran past it, I could see it so clearly. It became a powerful part of my healing journey.

I also meditated at least twice a day, without fail. Morning meditation became my daily ritual—I would wake up earlier just to do it. And I never missed a single day.

I used the Silva Method laboratory meditation to express gratitude, visualise perfect health, and cleanse my emotional, mental, physical, and spiritual bodies. I imagined dissolving negative beliefs, emotions, and any hidden issues in my body. These meditations became a powerful way for me to reset, focus, and fuel my healing from the inside out.

At least two or three times per day, I would sit quietly, go into a meditation, and visualise the doctors telling me that

I am clear from cancer, that my body is completely healthy, and imagine positive outcomes of my tests and appointments.

Or I would go for a walk or a run and visualise what I wanted to happen—my vision—focusing on the outcome: perfect health and how my life would look when I achieved it. The *what*, not the *how.*

Someone might call it daydreaming. For me, it was part of my visualisation practice.

Although I wasn't getting results immediately, it gave me the strength to get through and to keep my mind focused on health as the goal. I knew that it took time to get sick—and it would take time to get healthy again.

"The clearer you are when visualising your dreams, the brighter the spotlight will be to lead you on the right path."

Gail Lynne Goodwin

I approached my Angelic Reiki teacher and felt drawn to work with her throughout my healing journey. I also started exploring the emotional and spiritual causes of breast cancer.

I began journaling everything I was doing—my emotions, everything that was happening related to my diagnosis—especially because I felt like it had happened for a reason, and maybe one day I would share my story with other women. I knew I was going to write a book.

I had always wanted to write one but never knew what to

write about or how. But this was a game changer. The inner feeling was strong—that I was going to overcome all my fears of judgment, fears about English not being my first language, and all the other things that had stopped me from writing a book before.

I started to see the cancer as a gift—something I might be able to share one day with the world and use to help other women on this challenging journey.

Go the extra mile. It's never crowded.

DR. WAYNE D. DYER

Facing my own mortality

I felt deeply connected to myself, the Universe, God—or whatever we call the higher power. Although I wasn't religious, it felt right to start calling it God for the very first time. I felt connected to Mother Meera, Sai Baba as my spiritual guides, and the angels. It was as if the anxiety and uncertainty about the results of all my scans brought me closer to the spiritual realm. I wasn't sure whether the doctors would classify my condition as curable or incurable, and I felt close to death.

I often thought about death—what it is like to die, and what I hadn't done in my life if I were to die. Although I was on a mission and dedicated to healing, I had never felt such an inner sense of being so close to death. It was like something was mesmerising me, like somewhere deep inside I was fascinated by the process. Of course, I didn't want to die, but I felt the closest I've ever been to understanding that *if* it was my time, I could reach a place of acceptance.

It was something like a mystical experience—when I felt close, but also felt like I didn't belong there yet. My biggest concern, if I were to leave this world, was that Max would be looked after well.

I started to see and hear stories about survivors developing a strong relationship with a Universal power—their higher self, the Universe, or God. It doesn't matter what we call it; it is my belief that it's the same power and energy. People healed by putting their trust in the process of life—or in God.

This connection to a Higher Power (in whatever form) also helped some people I knew cross the bridge to the other side peacefully.

It came to my understanding that if I wasn't meant to recover, I wouldn't—and in that case, I felt the best thing would be to reach a point of acceptance.

The soul always knows what to do to heal itself.
The challenge is to silence the mind.

CAROLINE MYSS

IV

Between Final Diagnosis and Starting Chemotherapy

The week before the final diagnosis was an emotional rollercoaster. I cried often but also gained powerful insights. It felt like a deep emotional cleanse.

One of the biggest realisations was how breast cancer treatments affect a woman's femininity—removing or altering the breasts, causing hair loss (including eyebrows and eyelashes), and damaging nails. It felt like the treatments stripped women of their feminine traits, almost masculinising them. Studying the emotional and spiritual roots of breast cancer, I saw a parallel: something must break before it can heal.

At the same time, I felt excitement about the changes ahead—nourishing my body and mind, forming better habits, and letting go of past emotional baggage. I especially wanted to clear limiting beliefs that had affected my relationships, and I still held resentment from my previous job. I started questioning my purpose and felt a strong desire to use my career for a more fulfilling, balanced life—one with time to explore what truly brings me joy.

I sensed I was entering a major life transformation. I began to enjoy time with others more and saw how fragile life really is.

With the final diagnosis in hand, it was time to be pragmatic. I also wanted to enjoy the time I had before starting chemo, while I still felt well.

On Friday, 24th February, the day after receiving the diagnosis, I reached out to my future employer. I needed to decide whether to continue with the new role or consider staying in my current job, which offered income protection and private healthcare. I hoped to move forward—it felt like time for a fresh start.

Coincidentally, I already had a pre-onboarding call with my future manager scheduled that day. I messaged him early in the morning, saying I had important health news and wanted to discuss it during our call.

Later that morning, I also spoke with my financial broker about insurance tied to my upcoming job change. When I shared what was happening, he reminded me to check the critical illness cover on my mortgage. When I did, I was stunned to see I might qualify for a significant payout.

That gave me a sense of financial security. Since my diagnosis was treatable—not terminal—and didn't require extreme interventions, I no longer felt compelled to stay in my current job just for the safety net. With the potential payout, I felt more confident about taking the risk and moving forward with the new job.

Still, I waited for that conversation before deciding. I hadn't heard back before our 3:30 call, so I joined with my heart racing.

I opened the conversation by saying I wasn't sure if he'd

read my message—he hadn't. So I had to deliver the news directly. I told him I'd been diagnosed with breast cancer. Thankfully, it hadn't spread and was treatable, but I would need seven cycles of chemotherapy starting 10th March, followed by surgery and possibly more treatment.

I explained that I was comfortable taking on the new role—except for the unknowns around chemo. Everyone reacts differently, and I couldn't offer any guarantees. I wanted an open conversation, not focused on legalities but on mutual comfort with whatever decision we made.

His response blew me away. He stayed calm, said life happens, and that he still wanted me to join. He'd speak to HR and get back to me. I felt a wave of relief—but still wanted to hear from HR directly before letting myself exhale fully.

Then he offered to end the call, but I said I was okay to continue and to carry on with our planning for my start, team discussions, and the strategy. We finished the call just after 4 PM, and I didn't expect him to get back to me before the following week. Within a few hours, I received an email from my future manager. He had already spoken to the HR director, and nothing had changed from their perspective—they still wanted me to join. They just suggested I think about whether or not to share my diagnosis with colleagues and offered to set up a call with HR to discuss how best to navigate everything. I agreed, wanting to understand my options and support.

The company had promoted a culture of flexibility and work-life balance, and I genuinely looked forward to working there. That same day, I spoke with my current manager. I thanked him for offering to revisit my resignation but explained that, after much reflection and reassurance from the new employer, I'd decided to move on. I felt I needed the change—staying in the old environment wouldn't support my healing. Still, I was deeply grateful for the opportunity and support.

It turned out to be a good day. Despite everything, I felt like my life was still unfolding as planned. That felt like a sign.

The next day, 25th February, I wrote in my journal that I felt as though my soul had chosen this path to connect me with the right people to fulfil my purpose—especially in women's health, prevention, and healing.

On 26th February, I began using the Silva Method "Mirror of the Mind" technique to prepare for chemotherapy. I visualised the treatment affecting only the cancer cells and leaving the rest of me untouched. From that day forward, I committed to programming this outcome twice daily until treatment began.

Time was flying. I was still working, which gave me structure and helped maintain a sense of normalcy. Outside of work, I was in meetings with Klara about launching our property business. We focused on rent-to-rent serviced accommodation strategies, starting with landlord outreach and studying how to structure a company. The new job would help me save for a deposit to buy our first property.

I also continued attending Toastmasters to improve my public speaking—something I didn't want to give up, even now.

By 27th February, though generally organised, I started feeling overwhelmed by the volume of appointments and decisions. Sandra stepped in to help. With her project management skills, she set up a Trello board to track everything. I didn't call it "Beating Cancer." I named it *Journey to My Perfect Health*.

On 28th February, I joined another Silva Method meeting where I learned new healing techniques. I started using the Three Scenes Technique to visualise chemo working efficiently, shrinking tumours with no side effects, and me still enjoying life.

For 2nd March, I marked "Fun Day" in my journal. That morning, I used meditation to set the tone—and it worked. I had two appointments in Cambridge, and the day was surprisingly joyful.

The highlight was my wig fitting at Maggie's. It was, oddly enough, one of the most fun moments in the entire journey. I tried on so many styles and couldn't decide. I called Sandra for her opinion. I loved a wavy, mid-length option, but its dark roots made me hesitate. Then the lady mentioned most wigs can't handle heat styling. That tipped me toward another one: a long, thick platinum blonde wig that could be curled or straightened. I'd just bought curling tongs before my diagnosis and figured I might finally use them—though, in the end, I never did. Still, the choice felt right.

The wig didn't look anything like me—and that's what excited me. I had so much fun during that appointment.

Afterwards, I walked through Cambridge to a lovely vegan restaurant for lunch, then returned to the hospital for the research biopsies. The radiologist was amazing—she numbed the area so well, the procedure barely hurt, for the first time ever. I'd visualised a fun day, and that's how it turned out—even with biopsies. I felt like I was in the saddle again.

Friday, 3rd March—I woke up feeling overwhelmed. I was trying to hand over everything at work and didn't want to let anyone down, especially the new colleague I was supposed to manage. I knew it wasn't my fault, but I still felt bad.

What I really needed now was time—to get organised, reset, and enjoy the days before chemo began.

That day, my mum arrived from Slovakia to support me through treatment. She doesn't speak any English, but she came without hesitation. She's truly an angel, and I'm lucky to have her.

I signed off from work, visited my brother's family to celebrate my nephew's 2nd birthday, then picked up Mum from Stansted. Since we were close to London, we stopped at IKEA for a few bits—I mainly wanted a headboard with shelves for my bed, so that when I'd be recovering from chemo, I'd have a calm room with everything I needed nearby.

On Saturday, 4th March, Mum and I had a nice lunch and spent most of the weekend putting the headboard together. I finally mounted the new shoe cabinets that had been sitting around for weeks. I decided to be brave and drill through the wall near the kitchen, having borrowed a pipe and cable detector from my friend Ed. It all worked out (and the cabinets are still there without any damage to electricity). Phew!

In my Sunday, (5th March) meditation I saw big brown bubbles in my aura and believed in the healing process as I could see them getting smaller.

I wrote in my journal in my week review:

Try/Learn something new	*How to store my Vitamin V*
I am excited about	*My healing journey*
Big wins/What made me happy	*I will be able to help people with cancer. And my new wig.*
Lesson learned	*Transformational time & Exciting*

In the Health & Fitness section of my goals, I wrote: "Boost my liver, kidneys, immune system." Under Quality of Life, I put: "Enjoy life & every day & be happy."

No wonder people around me thought I'd lost it—but really, it was just a shift in mindset. I was no longer a victim. I was taking control.

Tuesday, 7th March was my last day at the office. I went in for a half-day—had some final handover meetings, and met for coffee with my coach and his assistant to talk about continuing our sessions once I transitioned into the new role. I also shared my health news. Then I had lunch with my friend Ellie before heading to Cambridge for a visit with the Chinese herbalist, ahead of starting chemotherapy.

That evening, I joined a call with Silva Method graduates and our instructor, deepening my understanding and practice. It had been a full, busy day—just how I liked it—but I knew I now needed more stillness and space to prepare.

Wednesday, 8th March, I had another call with my future manager to discuss strategy and how I could best contribute once I joined. Since I hadn't yet heard from HR, I reminded him to follow up. He promised to arrange a call.

Thursday, 9th March, I began preparing physically for chemotherapy. I applied dark red nail varnish—a colour I'd never normally wear, but dark polish helps protect nails from UV damage during chemo.

I also went to the hairdresser to cut my hair into a shorter bob. I was planning to try the cold cap to reduce hair loss, but I hate the cold and wasn't fully committed. I didn't go too short—I still wanted to feel like myself, at least while I had my hair.

That haircut also served a purpose: I was raising funds for

the Little Princess Trust, which makes wigs for children facing hair loss. I was amazed to learn that it takes 14 hair donations to make just one wig. In the end, I raised over £500.

That night, I focused on visualisations and spiritual connection. The next day was a big one—my first chemotherapy session.

V

Chemotherapy

I had seven chemotherapy sessions planned, one every three weeks. The first four were Docetaxel, combined with a targeted injection called Phesgo (Herceptin and Perjeta). The last three were a mix of EC chemo drugs—Epirubicin and Cyclophosphamide—often called the "red devil."

The plan was treatment, recovery, and a gradual return to normal before each next cycle. I briefly reviewed the potential side effects of Docetaxel—everything from fatigue, nausea, and hair loss to nerve issues and skin changes. EC came with its own list: bladder irritation, red urine, liver strain, and more. But I reminded myself that side effects vary from person to person, and the only thing I could truly control was my mindset. So I focused on visualising a smooth process with no side effects at all.

The hardest part was knowing I felt completely healthy—but was about to deliberately make myself unwell.

My first chemotherapy

Day 1 – 10th March

The day began with uncertainty. I had so many questions: Would I react badly? Would I feel sick? How long would it last?

I started the morning with meditation and visualisation. I imagined the chemo going directly to the cancer cells, sparing the rest of my body, and me still feeling well and active.

Eventually, I decided to surrender to the process, trusting that I was in the safest place—hospital—if anything went wrong.

I packed for the day: snacks, a hot water bottle, something to read and listen to, and tools for meditation. Lisa, a kind friend from work, picked me up. It had started snowing heavily that morning, but thankfully the journey was smooth.

Mum stayed home with Max, my cat. She doesn't speak English, and we agreed it would be too stressful for her if something went wrong—no one would be able to explain what was happening.

At the hospital, Lisa stayed with me through the entire appointment and would take me home afterward. I was nervous about returning to the oncology unit—my first visit had been emotionally overwhelming. But this time, the atmosphere was calm, not daunting at all.

My appointment was at 11:30. I received steroids and antihistamines first, to prevent nausea and allergic reactions. The nurse, Raquel, was lovely—she explained everything clearly and with care. When it was time to try the cold cap, she asked me to apply a generous amount of conditioner to my hair.

They brought over the cap—it looked like a helmet on a wheeled stand. I wet my hair, added conditioner, and Raquel fitted the cold cap snugly over my head.

As soon as the cold cap was placed on my head, the freezing pain was immediate and intense. I tried distracting myself by talking to Lisa and the nurse, but it felt unbearable. The nurse reassured me that it usually gets better after ten minutes, but within the first two, I knew I couldn't go through with it. I asked them to take it off. I understood this meant my hair would likely fall out, but I couldn't imagine enduring that kind of discomfort every session—especially for something that only works 50–70% of the time and might leave patchier results than just going bald.

Next came the Zoladex injection to temporarily shut down my ovaries and block oestrogen. It was injected into my stomach and would be repeated at each chemo session. Then I received the Phesgo injection—targeted therapy for HER2-positive cancer—administered into the fatty tissue in my thigh.

The antihistamines made me very drowsy, so the nurses advised me to monitor how I felt and report any symptoms. Then the Docetaxel infusion began. Apart from my hands feeling a little cold, I didn't feel anything. I closed my eyes and visualised the medicine going only to the cancer cells, healing me.

Lisa stayed by my side the whole time—letting me chat or sit quietly as I needed. The steroids gave me a huge energy boost, and I ended up talking most of the appointment. I was incredibly grateful for her time—driving me, staying with me for hours, and taking me home.

While the drip was running, the nurse came over with

a list of medications I needed to take home. That moment overwhelmed me. As someone who barely takes any medicine, it was a lot—strange names, unclear instructions. I tried to make notes but knew I'd need to create a better system to manage it all.

They also gave me another red Rapid Response Card with a number to call if I felt unwell, had a fever, or noticed any worrying symptoms.

I had feared the oncology unit would feel heavy and depressing—but I was wrong. It was clean, bright, and incredibly well run. The nurses moved like bees in a hive, focused, efficient, and kind. Despite how busy it was, the whole atmosphere was calm and uplifting. Even the patients seemed at peace.

Lisa and I had both expected me to leave feeling sick or drained—but I felt fine, buzzing even. We chatted the whole way home like nothing had happened.

Back home, though, I noticed the effects of the steroids. My mind was racing, my body both tired and wired. I felt oddly impatient and restless, especially around my mum. It was like I was on fast-forward and she was moving in slow motion.

To stay on top of things, I rewrote my medication schedule into a calendar hanging in the kitchen, next to where I kept my supplements. I also looked for a good tracking app but couldn't find one that suited me.

Later, I joined the Silva Graduate Healing Group online. We sent healing to each other and loved ones. It felt powerful—I could feel the energy flowing through me. It did me a lot of good after such a full day.

During the healing session, I started to feel nauseous,

with brain fog and a dry mouth. I didn't feel like eating or drinking but managed a few sips of water. It was strange—my mind was buzzing from steroids, yet clouded at the same time. Still, I eventually fell asleep.

In the middle of the night, I woke with stomach cramps and thought I'd have diarrhoea—but I didn't. My tummy settled, but my mind was racing. I had a flood of ideas, opened my laptop, and typed for a while before falling back asleep.

By morning, the cramps returned, and I felt awful—like a severe stomach bug. I wasn't sure if I was going to faint, vomit, or both. While on the toilet, I passed stool but became dizzy, saw only darkness, and heard loud ringing in my ears. I was terrified.

I asked my mum to bring me the Rapid Response card from the fridge—a lesson learned, as I hadn't saved the number and couldn't get it myself. She also brought a cold towel for my neck, which helped. Once I could see clearly again, I called the hospital. The nurse explained it was a common chemo reaction and advised taking anti-sickness medication before feeling ill, not after. I made a mental note—and saved the emergency number in my phone.

Day 2 – 11th March

I stayed in bed most of that morning. The ear ringing lingered, and I felt weak, but I managed to take my meds, drink fresh juice, and eat crackers and banana in bed. After more cramps around 9 AM, I passed stool normally again.

Despite everything, I remained mentally sharp—likely from the steroids—and did some work from my laptop, organising tasks and catching up. Later, I meditated and had a powerful spiritual experience. I felt connected to my guides, sensed emotional healing around past relationships, and received insights: eat smaller meals more often, and sleep with my upper body elevated.

I journaled these thoughts and outlined content for my journey. After a shower, I went for a 5–6 km walk, then helped Mum prepare lunch. I craved carrot and parsnip purée. After lunch and another steroid dose, Mum gave me an immune-boosting injection. My friend picked me up around 2 PM, and we walked another 3–4 km.

By evening, I was a bit tired, but amazed by how much energy I had. I'd walked 10 km, done housework, talked non-stop, gardened, and written—buzzing from the steroids. Eventually, I let myself unwind.

Later, I felt both nauseous and hungry, with a very dry mouth. I ate a little fruit cake and more puree, but felt full quickly. I took more anti-sickness tablets and went to bed, propped up—which helped with nausea. I slept well until just before 5 AM, when I woke with a sudden bowel movement.

Day 3 – 12th March

Sunday was the first day without steroids. I still felt nauseous but less than the day before. I decided not to take any more anti-sickness pills. I had a beautiful meditation and saw some guides and spiritual beings holding my hand in a circle that morning. It felt like they were guiding me through chemotherapy. I felt a very strong energy that didn't move—it stayed with me the whole time, and I felt it was still with me, guiding me through the entire chemotherapy journey.

We were then sending a lot of clearing to the planet, to

people, and to all the root causes of cancer. Then I felt like my heart opened to unconditional love. The meditation ended with me feeling deeply connected to Divine energy and to my life purpose. I felt like all is well in my life, and that I love myself.

For breakfast, I had two different juices along with all my natural supplements, then a small lunch. I still had cravings for the parsnip and carrot purée. I ate my lunch in phases and had very small portions more often. My friend picked me up in the afternoon and we walked 9 km together. I came home very tired but still did a bit of gardening and then had a lazy, early night.

Day 4 – 13th March

I woke up early in the morning with diarrhoea, feeling nauseous and dizzy. I had a terrible headache and felt like someone had been hitting me on the head the entire night. I also had a swinging sensation in my head. It felt like the worst hangover ever. It was as if, after those two very active days, it all hit me at once.

I decided to get some fresh air and went out for a walk. I had barely walked a couple of minutes when I realised I didn't feel stable on my feet and wasn't sure if I was going to pass out. I returned home within five minutes and went back to bed. From there, I managed to do some admin work and make a few phone calls, setting up a little "bed office."

I sorted out a refund for our theatre and Royal Ascot tickets—plans I originally made with Klara but had to cancel due to the chemotherapy. I also opened a travel insurance claim for my upcoming trip to Slovakia to visit my family, which I was now no longer able to do.

Before lunch, I laid down for a guided healing meditation and had a small nap. I managed to eat a light lunch and then went back to bed again.

Around 3 PM, I started to feel slightly better and decided to meet my friend for a short walk after she finished work, just before our scheduled property meeting. I came downstairs and noticed an email from the HR Director of my future employer. I felt a flicker of hope—she had been due to reach out to discuss how they could support me during my cancer treatment.

But as soon as I opened her message, I had a very bad feeling. The email read:

"Are you free this afternoon for a call? I need to discuss the Head of Product role with you asap."

It didn't feel at all like the supportive message I was hoping for. My stomach dropped. I instantly felt worse—now more emotionally than physically. My body felt like it went into spasm. My nausea deepened, but this time it wasn't just from the chemo; it was emotional.

I replied that I was available all afternoon and went out to meet my friend for our walk. As we walked, my phone rang. It was the HR Director. I answered, and she told me she was afraid she had bad news—they were withdrawing the job offer.

There I was, at the very start of an extensive cancer treatment plan, suddenly left without a job and no income. It felt like a bombshell. A bad dream I couldn't wake up from.

I tried to argue that this was illegal—that the job offer was being withdrawn only after I disclosed my diagnosis. But she wouldn't share any details and insisted it had nothing to do with the cancer, claiming it was due to a company restructure that also affected other people. I told her I would be seeking legal action and expected a detailed explanation.

I wasn't sure whether this moment was even more terrifying than the cancer diagnosis itself. The existential fear of losing my security, of potentially losing everything I had built, was overwhelming. I was suddenly thrown into a void of uncertainty—how could I find a new job while undergoing chemotherapy?

The first person I called was my current boss. I couldn't say much—just told him what happened. He was the first person I shared this news with, aside from the friend who had been with me when I got the call. I didn't have to explain; he understood instantly. He told me he would get back to me.

I got back home, and I think the shock of what happened suppressed all side effects—I no longer felt the awful headache and nausea. My mum came home from shopping, and we all sat in the living room, shocked and without any words. My friend and I tried to look for some legal help, and I was trying to get advice. I called my former colleague and friend to ask for guidance and tried to be pragmatic, but it was so stressful and worrying that I didn't know what to do. I couldn't sleep thinking about it all. I had to ask my mum—probably for the first time since childhood—to lay next to me in bed and hold my hand. I was so scared, completely devastated, thinking about how I was going to pay for everything. I was trying to find out how much in benefits I would get, and it wouldn't even cover all my bills. I knew I had the insurance claim, but I couldn't be sure if they would pay out at that stage. I managed to fall asleep maybe around 2 a.m., but didn't sleep well at all.

That Monday was the worst day of the whole cancer

treatment—not only because of how I felt physically, but how I felt mentally. I told myself that I wasn't rejected but redirected in life and that it happened for a reason. But I couldn't see how it could help me at that time. I hoped I could stay with my old employer for a bit until I got myself sorted, or until I received the insurance payout, or figured out another way to manage my living situation.

Day 5 – 14th March

I felt better, with less headache despite the lack of sleep and at least three episodes of diarrhoea. I realised that days 3 and 4 were the worst because I no longer had steroids to boost my energy, and the shallower, shorter sleep I'd had while on them had taken its toll.

My dry mouth was getting much worse, and my mouth became much more sensitive. Food that wasn't even spicy tasted spicy; mildly spicy food tasted extremely spicy, and one clove of garlic in a dish tasted like five. It felt good just to have a piece of watermelon in my mouth—I wished I could keep it there all day.

I received an email from the HR director stating that she needed to tread very sensitively and that she accepted the timing of their change was awful, but she wanted to inform me before internal changes began. I replied very angrily that it was not about "awful timing," but absolutely unacceptable behaviour—and I threatened to take legal action. I also started applying for jobs.

Later that day, I had a remote session of spiritual healing arranged, and there was a lot of clearing going on. We went back to my childhood traumas—clearing feelings of abandonment, my stay in the hospital as a child, my fear of war when I was six and my parents were involved in the Velvet Revolution. We worked on clearing my other fears, cutting ties with the past, healing past hurts, addressing my relationship with my dad, and bringing forgiveness to my heart. The session concluded that I was safe and protected when I was little—fearing the war—and that I was also protected during the cancer and the job loss. I felt again that it happened for a reason, though I still couldn't quite work out why.

Also, the brown bubbles in my aura that had been shrinking during a previous meditation completely disappeared in this session, as seen in my mind's eye. The session helped me greatly in finding some level of peace in tackling the uncertainty of job loss.

Later, I joined the Silva Method graduate group to surround myself with more positivity.

"You are never rejected, only redirected."

CATRIONA GRAY

Day 6 – 15th March

I woke up in the middle of the night due to another bowel movement. I took two tablets to relieve it, but they didn't seem to help much. I felt better in the morning, and for the first time, I sat behind the wheel and drove myself to the hospital for a cardiology appointment at 9:30. I felt a little bit zoned out and had to pay more attention than usual while driving. Maybe it was too early for me to drive after the chemo. My heart scan went okay and looked fine.

I felt better on the way back, and my mum and I decided to stop in Ely on the way home from the hospital. We went for lunch at Prezzo, as it was a weekday and not too busy. I really enjoyed the lunch—it felt like a return to normality. After that, we went food shopping before heading back to the car.

The main thing bothering me that day was the diarrhoea. Luckily, I didn't have an episode the whole morning, but then it hit me suddenly in Ely—fortunately close to a toilet. I couldn't wait for this side effect to go away. It wasn't like normal diarrhoea. It was more like randomly appearing episodes of loose stool, which was manageable at home but not so good when out and about. I was getting very anxious about it.

When we got back home, I received a phone call from my manager. He said that my employer was very sorry about what happened with my new job but that they would be happy to extend my notice period by three months, until mid-June, to help them with a few projects. This was fantastic news. Not only were my living costs covered for the next three months, but I was also assigned to specific projects, which removed the pressure and stress I had previously experienced at work. It was a win-win situation, and I was happy I could help them just as they were helping me. I felt blessed again.

I was told there might be a chance to continue working on a contractual basis after my notice period, and I noted in my journal that maybe life was steering me toward starting my own business.

After the call, I went upstairs to change and, instinctively, touched my breast—something I did often to check the tumours. At first, I thought I was imagining it, but I couldn't find the second tumour. I called my mum, and she said the same. The one behind my nipple also felt smaller. It was mind-blowing.

Only six days into chemo—after just five full days—I was already seeing results. I'd been told changes would appear after two or three cycles, not this soon. But I believed the recovery had started long before my first chemo on 10th March. It began the day after my diagnosis, when I shifted my mindset and cleaned up my diet. And something shifted the day after my spiritual healing with Mel, when I released long-held childhood traumas. That moment marked a profound turning point. I believed everything I'd been doing—emotionally, spiritually, and physically—must have been working in harmony with the treatment.

Day 7 – 16th March

I woke with diarrhoea, which lasted through the morning. By lunchtime, it eased, and I went for a walk with Klara. Halfway through, I felt cramps and desperately needed a toilet. I tried running home but didn't make it. It was humiliating—my worst chemo-related experience. It shook my confidence and made me fearful of leaving the house. I share this because I know other women must experience this too and feel just as embarrassed.

I stopped taking anti-diarrhoea meds and instead tried warm turmeric water and organic probiotics. My mouth remained dry, and watery vegetables brought the most relief at dinner.

Day 9 – 18 March

I wondered if the diarrhoea was caused by the anti-fungal tablets I'd taken from Day 5–7, since I had no bowel movement at all. The dry mouth, however, continued.

My brother's family visited, which lifted my spirits. Later, I had a call with Lisa who helped me file a claim with the Employment Tribunal against the company that withdrew their offer.

Day 10 – 19 March

I journaled in the morning, then went for my first run. Oddly, I felt safer running than walking—probably because I could get home faster if needed. I managed 5 km. It was tough, but possible, and I felt proud.

Later, I took my mum to the seaside. We went to Hunstanton, walked along the beach, and soaked in the sun and sea breeze. I wore my wig, sunglasses, and a big summer hat—things I wouldn't have worn before. But I felt confident and free. We had coffee and ice cream and got home by 5:30. It was an amazing day. I felt truly alive.

Day 11 – 20th March

I took it easy, as I had kept two days of my originally planned annual leave, so I was off on Monday and Tuesday. My loose stools were getting better, I felt better, had no cramps—but still had a dry mouth, which was quite annoying.

I also cancelled my travel insurance claim, as I managed to get a full refund on my flight tickets to Slovakia from the airline. I was surprised, but the airline refunded it based on my diagnosis. This meant I didn't have to pull together a lot of documents for the travel insurance claim, and it took me minutes to get my money back instead of weeks or months.

I still kept my flight tickets to Ibiza in June, just in case something unexpected happened and I could make it to my 40th birthday celebration.

Day 12 – 21st March

I was still off work, and the spring weather was lovely. Mum and I met a friend for lunch at a cosy Italian restaurant in the village. The food felt homemade and comforting. Later, I had a session with my Chinese herbalist in Cambridge. Her treatment room always transported me—it felt like a peaceful retreat in Asia.

Afterwards, we browsed a health food shop. My new diet was still fresh, and I enjoyed reading labels and discovering clean, nourishing options. I felt good overall, but indigestion crept in later that day.

Day 13 – 22nd March

I worked all day and looked forward to joining my Toastmasters group remotely. They'd arranged it specially so I could stay connected, and I truly appreciated it. The meeting went until 9:30 p.m.—a long day—and I wasn't sure I'd manage that schedule again.

Day 14 – 23rd March

I had a DEXA scan in the morning to check bone density—something I later learned is done at the start of chemo for long-term monitoring. I'd had two loose stools earlier, including one en route, so I took anti-diarrhoea meds more for peace of mind.

The hospital was in a beautiful, modern building, and the scan took only a few minutes. On the way home, we stopped in Ely for fresh fish and lunch. I had a goat cheese sandwich and a decaf coffee with plant milk—goat cheese being a small indulgence when eating out.

Back home, I worked and later went for a short walk with a friend. I also filled out a form for additional financial support. The best part of the day: no indigestion or dry mouth. A few breakouts showed up on my face, but that was minor.

Day 15 – 24th March

I worked through the day, then headed out for a longer run—about 7 km—along the fields where I visualised storing my "Vitamin V." I felt ready for it.

Before the run, I received an unexpected email from the

person who was meant to be my new manager before the job offer was withdrawn. He explained he'd been made redundant just days before, and that the decision wasn't personal. He expressed genuine regret and offered to talk.

We spoke during my run and had a great conversation. We both agreed we would've enjoyed working together and hoped our paths would cross again.

After my run and shower, I noticed hair starting to fall onto the floor—not in patches, but thinning noticeably. Everyone's experience is different, and mine was beginning.

Day 16 & 17 – 25th March & 26th March

We had a relaxing weekend with my mum, went for a walk to get some twigs to put in a vase as Easter decoration because that is a Czech tradition. I bought some flowers as well. We did Easter decoration at home and baked a homemade vegan bread from oats, without gluten, preservatives, or sugar. It turned out tasting like a cake. I was pleased with it. I stayed active and went for a run both days. I still had a loose stool a bit and started my period—likely the last one.

Day 18 – 27th March

I went for a blood test that needs to be done a few days before the next chemotherapy to make sure the treatment can proceed. I worked the whole day, working on different projects, which I enjoyed so much more than all the stress I had in my role before. I had a very productive day. I managed to do a 5 km run and walk by the river and finally sent my hair that I cut before chemo to the Little Princess Trust charity.

Day 19 & 20 - 28th & 29th March.

My blood test result revealed low haemoglobin, which was a sign of my iron deficiency anaemia, and I started to think if my iron levels dropped again. I managed to get an interview in a different company as well. My hair started falling out more and my parting became wider. I continued staying active and running, whilst also enjoying some downtime watching telly with my mum in the evening.

I heard from the insurance company regarding my claim, and they requested a medical form to be filled in by the GP. I started to question whether I filled my medical form correctly when applying for the insurance a couple of years back. But I spoke to my financial advisor, and he said he would send me the form I submitted when applying.

Day 21 – 30th March

I went to meet my two friends and colleagues as they wanted to hand me over my leaving presents. It didn't feel right for me, as I hadn't left the company at that time because they extended my notice period. However, they insisted that I should take them anyway so that I could enjoy them. And they were all very lovely, very cheerful, and to my liking. I said that it was someone who knows me well who chose all these presents. I also got beautiful pots with plants for outside, and these were another beautiful boost of positivity anytime I stepped into my garden.

After lunch, I took more steroids in preparation for the next chemotherapy. The time was up—chemo cycle 1 was complete. Cycle 2 was awaiting the next day.

My second chemotherapy

Day 1 – 31st March

I didn't sleep much as the steroids I took the day before kept me awake at night. But I woke up and had a very strong spiritual experience in my morning meditation. I saw vivid images of my morning meditation in preparation for chemotherapy and I felt like it was channelled through me and decided to record what I was seeing so that I could create healing meditations for other people with cancer.

To download the meditation and for more resources, please visit www.lotus-journey.com/book-bonuses

Shelley gave me a lift to Cambridge hospital. I expected my appointment to take only a couple of hours based on the information I was given last time, but they were short of staff, so it took over 3.5 hours.

All went well, and I got back home after 2:30. First, I got myself organised and put all the tablets I need to take—and when—into my calendar, and set reminders for other appointments and things I needed to do, such as booking another blood test at the GP in two weeks' time. Then I had lunch at 15:30.

I was still buzzing after the steroids, and again I felt very impatient and nervous when my mum asked me something. I literally felt a bit high from the amount of steroids combined with antihistamines and the chemotherapy.

As I was still active, I decided to make another carrot and

parsnip purée that I craved during the first chemotherapy cycle, so that I would be ready.

After the lesson I learned during the first chemotherapy, I took an anti-sickness tablet in the evening to prevent the awful sickness from happening again, and I joined the Silva Method healing group. This helped me relax and focus on healing—not only my own, but other people's as well. It was like a one-hour virtual retreat every time.

Later that night, I felt nauseous and took another anti-sickness tablet. I started having more frequent bowel movements during the night.

Day 2 – 1st April

I couldn't sleep much again—it was like my mind was buzzing all night. So I retyped the meditations I recorded on Friday morning and got them ready for a voiceover so I could then create a video on YouTube.

I was active the whole day but tired from the lack of sleep. I went for a walk and did a few guided meditations and Angelic Reiki self-healing, which was a great source of comfort and helped me feel more at peace while recovering from chemo.

I was getting hungry and planned to have the carrot and parsnip purée I had prepared, but I couldn't even smell it. I craved something bread-like instead. We baked a healthy version of buckwheat focaccia, which was more like a pizza base but with rosemary—and it was very nice. I wasn't eating much; I ate half of my lunch and had the leftovers for dinner.

I took it easy and we watched some series on the telly in the afternoon and a film in the evening. As the day went on, I developed a headache and felt pressure in my forehead. I also started having a dry mouth again. So I had an early night and finally slept well.

Day 3 – 2nd April

I woke around 5 AM, meditated, and went back to sleep. After another wake-up at 7, I felt low on energy, likely from the poor sleep over the past two nights. I stayed in bed and watched a property course.

After lunch and a short nap, I felt better. I went on a 7 km walk with a friend, did some gardening, and refreshed the indoor flowers. My dry mouth made me crave something fresh, so I had a light dinner: salad with watermelon, cucumber, and strawberries, and a slice of homemade bread. I felt chilled after dinner, went to bed early with a hot water bottle, and slept well.

Day 4 – 3rd April

Day 4 was again the worst—same as last cycle. I managed to function, but had a bad headache, brain fog, nausea, and felt like I was moving in slow motion. I kept taking anti-sickness meds, but still felt queasy and unable to nap despite fatigue.

Midday, I reviewed my critical illness insurance form and realised I had answered "non-smoker" when I'd only quit recently. The form defined a non-smoker as five years smoke-free. Since I'd also vaped, I panicked—worrying it would void my claim. I felt crushed. For the first time, I was close to receiving money that could change my life, and now it felt like I might lose it. I beat myself up for not reading carefully and grew anxious about what my GP records might show.

I went for a walk, but the anxiety stayed. The timing felt cruel—first the job offer withdrawn on Day 4 of cycle one, now this. I spent most of the evening in bed, watching TV. I ate okay, but again needed fresh food to soothe my dry mouth.

Day 5 – 4th April

I felt a bit better, but diarrhoea returned. I suspected the anti-fungal meds, though it could have been the chemo. When near a toilet it was manageable, but going out caused anxiety. I didn't tell anyone at the time—but I ordered adult nappies. It felt humiliating, but they gave me freedom and peace of mind on walks.

I also had a sore throat and pain in my right tonsil. I was tired and foggy, but organic guarana powder helped me power through work. The dose needed to be exact—it was potent.

Later, I joined an online call with the breast clinic about exercising during chemo and post-surgery. I half-listened at first, but was surprised to hear that studies showed patients who exercised—even on spin bikes during treatment—had better chemo outcomes. The advice had shifted. Where doctors once told patients to rest, they now encourage movement to support healing, recovery, and mental health.

It reminded me how outdated medical advice can be. What was once dismissed is now embraced. I believe this shift will keep happening—especially around things like diet. In many ways, patients must stay one step ahead.

I felt stronger mentally, so I set my mind to the fact that I have some control over what the GP fills in. I requested to see the form because I noticed there was inaccurate information—not just regarding my non-smoker status but also allergies and other things.

I spent the evening finishing the texts for the meditations I wanted to share with others who are going through cancer.

Day 6 – 5th April

I woke up feeling much better. I had a long day at work because I was helping with testing in the evening as well, so I took a nice small walk in the middle of the day. When I took another break at 4, I went for another short walk and then met online with Klara. Together, we set up a limited company and officially started our property business. I couldn't believe we actually did it—something that had been on my vision board and something we had spoken about for some time, we finally decided to make happen.

I realised we'd been talking about it and studying various property courses since the end of 2022. But now, while going through chemotherapy, we actually did it. It was a long day, but I felt like I was recovering much faster than I did after the first cycle.

Day 7 – 6th April

I worked the whole day and had a job interview, as well as a lot of other meetings. After work, my mum and I went shopping in Ely. I was wearing my wig for 11 hours, and my head was very itchy in the evening.

Day 8 – 7th April

It was Good Friday, and I enjoyed spending the time with my mum. I was still suffering from a dry mouth and tried all sorts of remedies, but nothing worked well for me apart from fresh, very watery vegetables and fruit, and plain meals without spices or too much garlic.

After several loose stools, I decided it was the right time to go out and try a run. I ran 4.3 km and felt great.

Later that morning, we tried making new desserts from avocado and vegan chocolate that didn't contain sugar, only coconut-based sweeteners. I was so pleased with the outcome—sweet, tasty, and healthy!

When I bent over to take some things out of the dishwasher, I had a very strange feeling when I stood back up. I suddenly felt like something in my blood dropped, and I felt dizzy for a while. I wondered if it could have been my iron levels again.

We spent the afternoon in the garden, planting vegetables and enjoying the yummy dessert while sitting outside. I also changed the layout of the lavender plants in my garden to make it look nicer. It was a nice, relaxing day at home.

Day 9 – 8th April

I felt nauseous in the morning, but my mum and I set off to meet my brother and his family at Audley End for an Easter train ride and walk. We spent the morning there. I was quite anxious about needing the toilet while being on the train, but luckily nothing happened. It was a very nice place, and it was great to see my nephew enjoying it so much.

Afterwards, my mum and I drove to the outlet in Braintree

to find a place to eat and do some shopping since we were close by. I had a very nice vegan katsu curry and two fresh juices, which did me good. My mouth was so dry I wished I could have been drinking the juice continuously.

I had planned to do some clothes shopping but ended up buying a food processor instead, to help with some of the new recipes I wanted to try after changing my diet. The shopping centre also felt like a safe place in terms of access to toilets—but I didn't need one after all. I was just anxious about it.

Although I experienced loose stools after this chemotherapy drug, it wasn't like regular diarrhoea. I never knew when it might happen—or how often. When it did happen, it was sudden, quick, and uncontrollable. Sometimes it happened three times in one morning; other times, just once a day, but at unpredictable times. That unpredictability was the most frustrating part. So, I usually wore a nappy and carried a spare set of clothes with me.

Day 10 – 9th April

We'd planned to have Easter lunch at my brother's, but they weren't feeling well, and I couldn't risk an infection. Mum and I stuck to our original plan to make a vegan, gluten-free nut roast. But the new food processor didn't work—we spent hours troubleshooting before realising it was faulty. It was frustrating and disappointing.

Thankfully, we managed to finish the nut roast without it, and it turned out delicious. I went for a run, and the rest of the day was quiet—lunch, gardening, and TV. My dry mouth and loose stools had improved, and side effects felt milder than in the first cycle. My hair was still there, but thinning steadily.

Day 11 – 10th April

On Easter Monday, I went for a morning run and then we drove to return the faulty processor. A road diversion took us through scenic countryside, which made the trip more enjoyable.

But just 15 minutes from the outlet mall, I had a sudden, urgent need for a toilet. At a petrol station, the assistant initially refused to let me in. I explained I was a cancer patient, almost in tears, before he finally relented. I was deeply upset by his lack of compassion.

We returned the processor, had coffee, and spent the evening comparing replacements online—eventually ordering a new one.

Days 12 & 13 – 11th & 12th April

I was back at work, with several meetings each day. My dry mouth worsened, and I had indigestion and a persistent feeling of fullness. Acne flared up again on my face.

Day 14 – 13th April

I was excited for my breast clinic appointment. It had been nearly a month since I first noticed tumour changes, and I was eager to request a scan to check progress.

I dressed up, put on my wig, and did my makeup. At the clinic, I asked if my mum could come in with me—she doesn't speak English, but I wanted her there for emotional support.

The surgeon said I looked well and asked about chemo. I told him it was going better than expected—I was still working and staying active most days. We then discussed the surgical plan, including the DIEP flap option (using tummy tissue for reconstruction). But I was overwhelmed and still hoping I might avoid surgery altogether.

I asked for an ultrasound to check progress, and he looked surprised. He explained that no scan was usually done at this stage. I told him I felt one tumour had vanished and the other had shrunk just five days after my first treatment. He seemed sceptical—but intrigued—and asked to examine me. Only then did I realise the appointment was meant to discuss surgery options, not scan progress.

He examined me and immediately sent the nurse to arrange an urgent scan because he admitted there was a significant change, and he wanted to see it for himself. He was amazed. He didn't accept anything I said about diet and mindset possibly being factors—he just said I had an amazing response to the chemotherapy and that there was a chance the cancer could clear before the operation.

Although I hoped the visible improvements meant I could avoid surgery, the surgeon explained that because the tissue had once been cancerous, it still needed to be removed. I was disappointed but understood.

He asked if I'd mind letting his students observe, saying I looked remarkably well for someone undergoing chemo. They came in, and he explained how patients can still live a full life during treatment. I found it funny, flattering even—and I was proud of how strong and positive I had become. Still, I hoped future treatments would be gentler than chemotherapy.

Although I expected an ultrasound, it wasn't originally planned. The radiologist was quiet at first, taking photos, while I visualised the tumours shrinking. Then she told me the inflamed lymph nodes now looked normal, one half of my breast was clear of calcification, and both tumours had shrunk significantly. She seemed genuinely happy to share the news, and I cried with relief.

I left feeling like a winner. Mum and I had lunch in Cambridge, did some shopping, and headed home.

Days 15 to 20 – 14th to 19th April

I'd been in touch with a recruiter and had a promising interview. A second round was scheduled, but the client went with someone else before it happened. The recruiter sent me a kind card after I shared what I was going through.

I felt low one day after lunch with a friend, who told me my ex was getting married. I wasn't upset about him—it was the right breakup—but it made me feel lonely. I'd been facing so much alone: low iron, chemo, side effects. I longed for someone to lean on. I was also discouraged about the job loss and uncertain insurance claim. But by the next day, I shifted my mindset—adding a sticker to my journal that read, "Be a warrior, not a worrier."

Life otherwise felt fairly normal. My stool was still loose but manageable. I kept running, though it got harder—like when my iron and haemoglobin levels dropped before. I chased up the oncology nurses about running new iron overload tests.

I also began having hot flushes, signs that chemo was pushing me into menopause. Sudden waves of heat hit me throughout the day, though sweating was minimal. I made light of it—after being known for always being cold, I joked I was finally warm.

Day 21 – 20th April

I went for my pre-chemo appointment. The specialist discussed my March heart scan, which showed fluid around the heart—but nothing serious, just something to monitor. Blood tests were also done during the visit.

My mum and I stopped off at a shop in Cambridge, and while we were there, I got a phone call from the oncologist registrar. She said one of my blood test results wasn't what they expected and that they had ordered a CT scan to find out what caused it. She said they would give me injections to prevent blood clotting, though she also mentioned it might be due to my supplements—which I didn't really buy into. Still, she said I needed to continue with the injections until the CT scan results came in.

I really didn't like the idea of taking injections I might not even need, so I was anxious for the CT scan to happen as soon as possible. They also recommended that I come to Cambridge hospital for my chemotherapy so they could do an ECG before treatment to decide whether it could proceed.

My iron levels were very low, and they planned to order both an iron infusion and the CT scan for the weekend.

I was a bit confused by everything I had heard but didn't think too much of it at the time. I was just pleased that it would all be sorted at the weekend. It was a bit tricky though, as I had to find someone who could be on standby to take me to and from the hospital over the weekend, since I wouldn't be able to drive myself while recovering from chemotherapy. But I accepted it—as long as it would all happen before Day 4, which had always been the worst day so far. I wanted my body to be strong enough to deal with it.

After that, we went for a nice lunch at a tearoom by the

river in Ely, did some shopping, bought vegetables and plants as usual, and then went back home.

I took steroids in preparation for tomorrow's treatment, which meant I didn't sleep much.

My third chemotherapy

Day 1 – 21st April

My chemo was scheduled for 10:30 in Cambridge. Klara gave me a lift, and I waited nearly an hour before starting. After an ECG came back fine, they gave me IV steroids and antihistamines. The treatment itself went smoothly, though the Friday clinic was packed, and everything took hours.

During the drip, I started organising my medication in Google Calendar. Since my blood results were raised and I was awaiting a CT scan, they gave me precautionary anti-clotting injections. I understood their reasoning, but treating a "maybe" felt excessive.

After treatment, I asked about my iron infusion and the CT scan—only to find no request had ever been made. I was told the iron infusion wouldn't happen Sunday as promised (they're closed), and there was still no update on the scan. I was frustrated, especially since I had to continue taking injections unnecessarily.

Already dealing with hot flushes and emotional swings—likely from hormonal changes—I now felt even more anxious due to the lack of follow-up. I'd flagged the iron issue two weeks earlier, and no one responded. I knew how badly low iron had affected me before, and the lack of support hit hard.

That night, I was nauseous, tired, and wired from the

steroids. I couldn't tell if I was hungry or sick, so I snacked. My mum noted my voice sounded cracked—just like after the last cycle.

Day 2 – 22nd April

The steroids kept me active. I took anti-sickness tablets and published my first meditation for chemo patients—something I felt proud of. I chatted with Sandra, cooked lunch with Mum, and later walked 11 km with Klara, including house steps. The rest of the day, I just relaxed and watched TV.

Day 3 – 23rd April

Lack of sleep caught up with me, so I napped before lunch. Later, I went for a walk, but I felt worse—more like Day 4, which is usually my lowest. I suspected low iron again and called the hospital, but the emergency line couldn't help. I felt helpless.

I went to bed early and woke repeatedly from thirst, drinking nearly half a litre at a time. At least I was sleeping deeply, and hydrating well helped flush the chemo.

Day 4 – 24th April

As expected, it was another rough Day 4. I felt exhausted, foggy, nauseous, had loose stools, and a pounding headache. I couldn't sleep, so I worked to distract myself. I'd started calling post-chemo Mondays my "blue Mondays," and this one was especially hard—made worse by low iron and no resolution in sight.

No amount of mindset work helped. I was overwhelmed

by frustration and fixated on feeling unwell, which only made things worse.

I tried to get in touch with the hospital, but as always, you need to leave a message with the nurses and wait for them to pick it up whenever they can. I couldn't wait any longer, so I called the hospital switchboard and asked to be transferred to the oncology day unit where they administer chemotherapy and also blood infusions. I managed to speak to someone there—they didn't have a date for me yet but said they were trying to arrange it, which at least felt like a step forward.

Later, I got a phone call from a nurse regarding my earlier query. They forwarded a request to the CT department, which was another issue that had been frustrating me. I was so fed up with the injections for preventing blood clotting. They were painful and horrible, and I hated putting something into my body that I might not even need. That just added to my stress.

Then I needed to print something, and the printer—of course—was acting up. Sometimes it doesn't connect properly and either needs another device to print from or a full restart of both the device and the printer. Well, it happened again, and I honestly thought I was going to smash the printer. I was so angry—I was screaming and shouting at the printer, at the cancer, at the hospital staff. I was furious and desperate. I hated the printer. I hated the cancer. I just wanted to be normal again.

I had a session booked with Mel, my Reiki teacher, but she had to reschedule—which was actually a good thing, because I wasn't in the right headspace. Later, when I did speak to her, I had a complete breakdown. It was probably the worst Day 4 after chemo so far. It was a combination of the chemo, low iron, the painful and possibly unnecessary injections and chemicals I had to take, and the menopausal symptoms like hot flushes and shifting hormones.

I did a meditation, and once my mind calmed a little, I realised I'd been in similar situations many times in the past—waiting for someone to do something, feeling unsupported, overlooked, and not paid enough attention. So I decided I had to really push and stand up for myself. I'd always worried about upsetting people or being punished for what I say. It took a crisis like this for me to finally do it. It felt very uncomfortable—and that discomfort added to my breakdown. I felt bad about myself for speaking up, but I did it.

Later that day, I received a call from the day unit saying they had booked me in for the iron infusion the next morning. The oncologist registrar I had spoken to before also rang me, apologised for the delay, and scheduled the CT scan for 28th April—four days away. I couldn't do much about the date, but I managed to negotiate with her to inform me as soon as the scan results are available, so I can stop the injections if they're not necessary. That was the main issue for me.

I was happy that the day was coming to an end. From previous rounds, I knew I'd start to feel better the next day—and that I would get the iron infusion first thing in the morning as well.

Day 5 – 25th April

I got up still feeling nauseous, but I was excited about getting an iron infusion. Klara was going to work in Cambridge and picked up me and my mum at 6:30. I had an episode of loose stool on the way to the hospital—luckily, we were just passing by a supermarket with a toilet.

When we got to the hospital, we waited for about 30 minutes. I asked for my mum to come with me, as I was feeling really down and wanted her there. They struggled to find my veins. It took several tries, which was quite daunting, but eventually they succeeded and the iron infusion went in. I felt much better knowing I would notice improvements within a day.

On the way back, we took a taxi. I suddenly had a craving for white bread—similar to sourdough—but specifically the kind I know from my own country. It's a different texture and taste than bread here in the UK, and for some reason, I was very specific about the type I wanted. We went to a shop and found a sourdough bread that was exactly what I had in mind. I came home and had it with vegan butter and jam made without refined sugar. I stuck to my diet as much as possible, though the bread did contain gluten and wheat, which I'd been trying to minimise. But in the grand scheme of things, I didn't feel like it would do any harm.

I worked for the rest of the day. My dinner was the same as my lunch. As usual, I ate half of my lunch at lunchtime and saved the second half for dinner—especially during the first week of each cycle. It was normal in the days after chemo to have specific cravings and fixate on one type of food for a few days. It was quite funny, especially as the cravings changed with each cycle.

I attended a Silva Graduate Zoom meeting but felt very nauseous—like I wanted to vomit, but didn't. This was followed by bad diarrhoea. I went to sleep after midnight but kept being woken up by bowel movements. I called the emergency line to check whether the iron infusion could have caused it, but they said it was probably a delayed reaction to the chemo. Maybe some internal processes restarted or were boosted by the infusion—who knows.

Day 6 – 26th April

I slept well but woke nauseous and had diarrhoea all morning, despite taking anti-sickness tablets. I worked to stay distracted. Strangely, I craved a croissant, and it actually helped settle my stomach—especially with dairy cheese and vegan butter. Later, I managed some sautéed vegetables, which felt warm and soothing.

I also had an issue with a wig I'd ordered weeks earlier. The colour was wrong, so I exchanged it, but the replacement—a yellow blonde—looked awful. The shop refused a second return, citing strict policies I hadn't noticed. I explained the colours were misrepresented, but they were unhelpful. My mum went out to buy more croissants, since that's all I could stomach. I ate one for dinner, worked a bit, and went to bed early.

Day 7 – 27th April

Still unwell. Recovery felt slower this time. I had a headache, dry mouth, nausea, and diarrhoea again in the morning—worse than the day before.

I managed a walk, then had a deep spiritual healing session with Mel. We uncovered lingering sadness from leaving Malta in 2022. I realised how deeply I miss the sea, and how much I crave the peace it brings. I wrote down that I need to build financial stability so I can live—or spend more time—there.

I also had a powerful reminder: divine energy isn't

something outside of me—it's within. Mel recommended *Dying to Be Me* by Anita Moorjani. I'd already bought the book just before my diagnosis but hadn't started it. That night, I finally opened it—and couldn't stop reading. I cried through much of it. It was raw, real, and deeply healing. I'd recommend it to anyone going through cancer.

Day 8 – 28th April

During my morning meditation, I clearly saw that I need to stand up for myself—whether it's about financial support or my insurance claim. I reflected on how often I've given away my power.

I kept thinking about Malta—what life would look like there—but also considered applying for British citizenship. I want to keep my base in the UK while exploring life elsewhere.

That day, I finally had my CT scan. I still wasn't feeling great and the process was rough. They had trouble finding a vein, and the injection was painful. Afterwards, my hand bled heavily and soaked the dressing within minutes. I had to wait while they stopped the bleeding before I could leave.

Afterwards, Mum and I went into Cambridge. We had a vegan wrap and a gluten-free crepe by the market, then stopped at a health food shop for some organic staples. On the way home, we swung by Ely's food market, but it was mostly greasy fast food, so we headed home to rest.

As the day went on, the dry mouth came back, which was very annoying.

Later that same day, I received a phone call from the hospital saying I could stop taking the injections because there were no blood clots. However, they told me they had found something that was putting strain on my lungs: pulmonary hypertension. To be honest, it didn't mean much to me at first. I just pictured that something was making it harder for my lungs to function. They said they'd book me in with the respiratory team. When I asked what it meant, they said it was treatable—with lifelong tablets. That was hard to hear. I don't like taking medication long-term, so I felt quite down about it.

Day 9 – 29th April

I woke up with loose stools again a few times in the morning but decided to go for a short run anyway. I ran 2.2 km and felt like that was enough. I no longer felt nauseous, but I had less appetite and still had a dry mouth.

The weather was nice, so I decided to take my mum to the seaside again. We spent the afternoon in Hunstanton. We took a lovely walk and had coffee and ice cream. I stuck to decaf coffee with plant milk and vegan ice cream. On the way back, we stopped in a shop and had a relaxing evening at home.

Day 10 – 30th April

It was a very similar day. I started with the usual loose stool in the morning, then went for a run—this time 4.5 km. We had lunch at home and set off to visit a Lavender Centre near the seaside. Afterwards, we ended up in Hunstanton again and played crazy golf.

Spending two days by the sea with my mum was exactly what I needed. It was refreshing and light-hearted—she even enjoyed playing a game she'd never tried before. Back home, we had a simple dinner and watched TV. I felt like myself again.

I also signed up for a challenge: walk 100 miles in May for Cancer Research UK. It gave me purpose and helped raise funds. Meanwhile, I continued reading the book *Dying to Be Me*—crying through it, but also healing. It shifted how I viewed cancer, my journey, and life itself.

Day 11 – 1st May

A bank holiday Monday. I woke feeling well, and the loose stools had eased. It was a sunny day, so I went for a longer run—7.5 km—and felt great.

Days 12 to 20 – 2nd to 10th May

The rest of the cycle went smoothly. Side effects were mild—mostly dry mouth and a few days of watery eyes. The prescribed medication for dry mouth didn't help much, but it was manageable.

I kept up daily runs of 4–5 km, which did wonders for both my mind and body. Running helped me feel normal, strong—even healthy—which is why I pushed myself to get back out by Day 6 after each chemo cycle. I followed the nurse's advice to avoid running for the first five days, but as soon as I could, I moved.

We had a lovely weekend celebrating King Charles's coronation—just me, Mum, and Klara, sharing lunch and a peaceful afternoon.

I also tried to sort out insurance paperwork. Unfortunately, my GP records still had outdated info about my smoking status. They couldn't change the official notes, so I contacted my former dentist. But their records were even older, suggesting I quit later than I had.

Back in 2021, I had proudly listed myself as a non-smoker when applying for the policy—I wasn't smoking or vaping at the time. But I didn't realise the definition required five full years of nicotine-free status, which I couldn't fully prove.

I found evidence that I'd registered as a non-smoker at a new dentist in 2020, and that I had switched to vaping years earlier, but nothing that proved I was nicotine-free since 2016. It was a toss-up—I did everything I could to support my case. I started visualising the money coming through and how it would feel, but also reminded myself: if it didn't come, I'd find another way to create it.

I also had a free legal advice session through Maggie's, regarding the job offer that was withdrawn. The lawyer found the timing of the company's restructuring highly suspicious and sent me a full summary and guidance.

Toward the end of the cycle, I noticed something unexpected: I was almost looking forward to the next chemo—not the physical effects, but the forced rest. I'd been so busy, constantly doing, seeing people, running errands. I realised I tend to push myself too hard. What I needed just as much as healing was to pause—to rest without guilt, enjoy stillness, and stop chasing tasks, goals, and obligations.

Day 21 – 11th May

The last day before chemo was my check-in with the oncologist. Sometimes it was just a phone call, but this time I was getting nervous because it was hours after the scheduled time and no one had called. I phoned the hospital, and they said I was still on the schedule.

One of my blood results—Alanine transaminase—showed a high level. I googled it (as you do) and found it could indicate liver issues, so I expected they'd say I couldn't have chemo the next day. But when the main oncologist finally called, they explained that the acceptable levels for chemo patients are different. What would usually be considered alarming is actually within range for someone undergoing treatment. It would have to be over 150 to be concerning. Looking back, I think I was probably just looking for a reason to refuse the treatment—I was getting fed up with it all.

The oncologist also explained more about the pulmonary hypertension and said it was treatable with lifelong tablets. I asked why it hadn't been picked up in the CT scan back in February, and she explained that it was a different type of CT—one without the contrast dye needed to highlight blood vessels—so they wouldn't have seen it. That made sense. She booked me to see a respiratory team on 6th September to discuss treatment.

I didn't want to be on lifelong tablets, so I started visualising all the blood vessels in my chest relaxing, releasing tension, and no longer under strain. I also began researching supplements used in Chinese medicine to support the respiratory system. I asked the Chinese herbalist I was already seeing, but she said to focus on the cancer and chemo first. So I took a different path.

I decided to take control. I researched Chinese herbs that had been trialled for pulmonary hypertension and found a few. And what did I do? I ordered them all and added them to my already long list of organic supplements. I was ready to try treating it naturally, and I planned to ask the doctors in September to monitor my condition while I used these herbal treatments—before agreeing to any lifelong medication.

I also asked about the research project I was supposed to be part of, but apparently it had been delayed.

I took steroids before my chemo the next day and, as usual, felt quite active afterwards. I tend to have more appetite after steroids, which is helpful because I can't eat much post-chemo—but the day before, I ate more than usual.

I was also looking into homeopathy, something I had wanted to explore early on but hadn't yet. I suddenly started coming across references to it often. I found out that it was covered by my employer's private healthcare, so I contacted a local homeopath that day. We connected really well and had such a nice chat on the phone. She said she had experience helping women with breast cancer and also mentioned incorporating angelic energy into the healing process. That resonated with me so deeply, the decision was easy—I booked in.

She asked me to put together a timeline of all my illnesses, health struggles, and major life events, which turned out to be a very interesting reflection exercise as well.

My fourth chemotherapy

Day 1 – 12th May

I woke at 5 AM—my mind racing from the steroids. This was my first chemotherapy session at the outreach centre in our village, just a 5-minute walk away. I'd been told treatments here would be quicker—2–3 hours—but like Cambridge, delays happened. Their computer system was down, and all other appointments that day were cancelled.

They struggled to find my vein (again), so we used my hot water bottle. This has always been an issue, made worse by frequent chemo and blood tests. In the end, my treatment took five hours, but the staff were kind and I felt lucky mine wasn't cancelled.

I chatted with a woman my age the whole time. We exchanged contact info and decided to stay in touch.

This was my last Docetaxel + Phesgo cycle. The next ones would be EC (Epirubicin and Cyclophosphamide), nicknamed the "Red Devil." The nurse said EC usually causes less diarrhoea—thankfully—but more nausea, so stronger anti-sickness meds are used.

Mum met me halfway home. Once back, I updated my Google Calendar with meds and timings. After dinner, I felt the meds clash—steroids energising me, antihistamines making me sleepy. I took probiotics and joined the Friday healing meditation before going to bed around 10 PM.

Day 2 – 13th May

I woke again at 5 AM, nauseous, with frequent stools. I stayed in bed doing Reiki and meditation. Later, I joined a session with the Cambridge Sai Centre. During that time, I focused on clearing blockages—around receiving health, abundance, guidance, and life itself.

A strong realisation came through: this journey has brought me closer to God—universal energy, the divine, or the Universe. I understood that everything happening is part of a bigger plan, and that stillness is essential to hear divine guidance. During meditation, I felt one of my spiritual guides healing my breast. It moved me deeply.

That day was also special because my friend Martina ran a 5K race for me back home.

Day 3 – 14th May

I slept better—maybe my body is adjusting to the steroids. I woke feeling swollen: puffy ankles, bloated stomach. The loose stools returned, and I hoped EC chemo would put an end to that side effect. I was tired of needing pads every time I left the house.

I spent the morning working from bed, then went for an 8 km walk to keep up with my 100 Miles in May challenge. I was exhausted afterward and rested the rest of the day.

Later, Mum and I took Max, our cat, for a walk in the garden—on a lead, since he's an indoor cat. I had an appetite, but still felt too full to eat much.

Day 4 – 15th May

Day 4—always the worst, and it was the same again. I slept almost the whole night, but it was very light sleep. I woke up with diarrhoea, a bloated tummy, and a really bad headache. This time, I didn't feel nauseous, but I still felt so full despite not eating much at all.

I worked again, just to keep busy so the day would go faster. But everything felt like hard work. I had brain fog and just didn't feel well. Things got a little better as the day went on.

Day 5 – 16th May

I didn't sleep well, waking several times during the night to go to the toilet. The bowel issues remained the most annoying side effect—perhaps second only to the dry mouth, though it wasn't as bad as in previous cycles.

I was tired but worked the whole day again. Everything still felt slow. I had a bad headache and felt like I was hungover. I also felt full in the afternoon, even though I hadn't eaten much, and experienced a new sensation—like something was sitting on my chest.

I rested after work and then went for a 30-minute walk. In the evening, I helped one of our Silva Method instructors during a class.

With this new cycle came new cravings. This time it was potato pancakes, but I didn't want the traditional kind, so we tried making sweet potato pancakes—which turned out really tasty.

Day 6 – 17th May

I slept well but still felt tired. I was supposed to have my first plastic surgery consultation, and Sandra was joining me. But an hour before, it got cancelled and rescheduled. I met Sandra in Cambridge anyway for coffee and a much-needed chat.

I felt emotional, still clinging to hope that surgery might be avoided. I was growing weary of the whole chemo process. I skipped dinner due to indigestion and dry mouth, had several bouts of diarrhoea, and bone pain in my pelvis and lower back. I went to bed with a hot water bottle. I also had a random craving for smoked salmon—but didn't act on it, and the craving passed.

Day 7 – 18th May

A restless night—woken repeatedly by bowel movements. I woke up nauseous, not sure if I was hungry or just sick. Still, my mindset had slightly improved.

Mentally, I was struggling. I felt frustrated, tired of chemo, and envious of those who had healed naturally. I didn't want to lose my breast or continue chemo. I believed in the power of lifestyle changes—I had already seen results—and I wanted to stop. But fear held me back. My belief in natural healing wasn't strong enough yet to take that leap.

I hoped they'd reduce my chemo rounds or cancel the surgery if the cancer was gone, but I already knew that wasn't likely.

That afternoon, I had my first homeopathy session. The calm in the room brought me to tears. We covered my health history and emotional trauma. I was tired of putting my body through this. I left with several remedies and a lighter heart.

Later, I went for my first run of the cycle, which helped lift my mood. That evening, I supported a Silva Method class and then went to bed.

Day 8 – 19th May

I felt better overall, though the diarrhoea continued—typical of this chemo type. I was relieved this was my final cycle with it. The dry mouth had also been irritating, and I looked forward to that subsiding.

I'd been taking indigestion tablets daily but decided to stop—they hadn't helped. I ordered activated charcoal to try something more natural and gentler.

That morning, I had an interview for a Head of Product role, which went well. I was anxious about my contract ending in mid-June and the uncertainty ahead. I had to schedule interviews during my better chemo weeks and make excuses to avoid the first-week fog. I even had to wear a pad during interviews in case of sudden diarrhoea—just another layer of stress. Thankfully, there were no incidents.

There was still a possibility of staying with my current employer—via contracting or part-time—but things were uncertain. My manager was working on it, but no decisions had been made yet.

Day 9 – 20th May

My friend Sandra did the Mighty Walk along the Norfolk coast for a cancer charity—and for me. She even painted a stone for me and left it on the beach during her walk. A deeply touching gesture.

It was a beautiful day, so I decided to take my mum to Sheringham Park, as we could borrow a scooter for her so we could easily get around without her knee being painful. It was a heartwarming feeling to know that Sandra was walking along the Norfolk coast—the same coast—and passing by Sheringham.

Sheringham Park is known for its rhododendrons, and they were all beautifully blooming, with lovely sea views. It was exactly what we needed. We spent maybe over an hour in Sheringham Park, as my mum could only get to certain places on the scooter. Then we drove into Sheringham and had a nice lunch at a Thai restaurant, later walked along the sea, and found a little café where we had cake and coffee.

I bought my mum a handbag, just because she had looked after me so well and was spending several months with me in a foreign country without speaking any English. She is my angel.

Day 10 – 21st May

We stayed home and just went to check the tyres and oil in my car and did some shopping in Ely. My birthday was coming up, and I was desperate to get out of my house—and out of Littleport, Ely, and the whole of Cambridgeshire. We waited until the last minute because I didn't want to book anything until I knew I felt better. Finally, after talking about it for a couple of weeks, I booked an apartment in York and decided to take my mum and myself to celebrate my 40th birthday.

Day 11 – 22nd May

We left early for my 9 AM breast clinic appointment in Cambridge, navigating heavy traffic and a packed car park. Thankfully, the clinic wait wasn't long.

I entered the room with butterflies in my stomach—I couldn't feel any lumps anymore and was hoping for good news. The radiologist was quiet, then finally said:

"The only thing left of the second tumour is the clip we inserted. Without it, I wouldn't know cancer was there."

The tumour behind the nipple was still present, though flatter. She called the results amazing and told me to enjoy my trip to York.

I was overwhelmed with emotion—one tumour gone felt like the best birthday gift. We returned home by 11 AM. I worked, went for a run, and did some gardening, feeling elated.

Day 12 – 23rd May

Side effects shifted—loose stools eased, but I had constipation and a hard stomach. Dry mouth persisted, and the feeling of fullness remained. I worked, went for a run, and packed for our trip to York.

We prepped juices and supplements, even bringing the juicer along. We'd booked an apartment with a kitchen so I could stick to my routine. That evening, my colleagues surprised me with birthday flowers—Ed even delivered them personally, despite living far away. It was a touching gesture.

Day 13 – 24th May (My 40th Birthday)

Mum and I drove to York and spent the day walking the city and enjoying lunch. After we checked into our lovely apartment, she rested while I walked York's historic city walls. It was a full and satisfying day.

Day 14 – 25th May

We explored York, took a windy boat trip, and had a celebration lunch. Mum treated me to a new wig as a birthday gift. Rain arrived later, so we headed to an outlet mall for indoor browsing.

Day 15 – 26th May

We checked out and drove to the coast near Scarborough. It was a beautiful sunny day—we had a picnic on a cliffside bench with a sea view and went for a walk before driving home.

On the way back, I started to feel anxious about my income. But then, unexpectedly, my manager called to extend my notice period by six months. It was a huge relief. I was still waiting to hear back from another company, but I began to think it might be best to stay where I was through the end of the year.

We got back home later in the evening, feeling full of joy about the lovely time we had. Also, the whole time we were in York, I only had dry mouth and lips and a feeling of fullness in the afternoons—so I went without dinner. But other than that, I felt absolutely fine the whole time.

Day 16 – 27th May

I celebrated my birthday with Klara at Ickworth House—one of my favourite National Trust places and a personal sanctuary. We walked, had a lovely healthy picnic she'd prepared, and later enjoyed a plant-based chocolate cheesecake back at home. I felt truly blessed. That evening, I prepped food for visiting friends the next day.

Day 17 – 28th May

I spent the day with Ed and Sarah. We had foil-baked salmon, tabbouleh, and nibbles—simple but enjoyable. We also finished off some leftover birthday cake and went for a walk. It was peaceful and grounding.

I'd been listening to more research on diet and cancer healing, which brought up internal conflict. I realised I still had doubts about my ability to heal naturally. I had joined a Facebook group focused on natural healing but left—it made me feel guilty for continuing conventional treatment and pushed me into a dark headspace.

This was the second emotional low in recent weeks. I didn't want more chemo, but I was afraid to stop. I asked the Universe for guidance and awaited results from the tumour profiling research, hoping it would give clarity on future treatments.

Days 18 to 20 – 29th to 31th May

Bank holiday Monday brought some much-needed rest. I finally unwrapped all my birthday gifts. Since coming back from York, I'd felt good—physically strong, running and walking daily. Only mild side effects lingered: watery eyes and minor nosebleeds, likely from lowered platelets.

I completed my 100 Miles in May challenge for Cancer Research and raised nearly £200—an incredible feeling during active treatment.

Day 21 – 1st June

At my pre-chemo oncology appointment, I ran into my old landlord, though he didn't recognise me. It was a sobering moment—he was there with his father, also battling cancer.

The results from the tumour research were in. I had expected treatment-specific insights, but it only flagged drugs my body may not tolerate—not whether my current or upcoming treatment would be effective. That was disappointing.

The good news: the cancer wasn't genetic. A relief, even though genetic cancers are rare.

I had also hoped that if the cancer disappeared during chemo, they would reduce the number of chemo cycles. But they told me they wouldn't do that unless I couldn't tolerate it. Otherwise, I'd need to complete the full number of cycles as a preventative measure. If the cancer disappears, it might mean fewer treatments afterwards, but not fewer chemo sessions.

We also discussed the other condition they found on my CT scan—pulmonary hypertension. I was told that it's a strain on the blood vessels and affects the lungs and heart. It also carries high risks for surgery and pregnancy. I was booked for an appointment on 6th September, where the respiratory team will measure the pressure. If it's too high, they'll put me on lifelong medication. If they find the cause of the hypertension, they might be able to treat that instead.

In the meantime, I was already taking supplements I had researched for this condition and was visualising a positive outcome for the appointment at the respiratory clinic.

I also started thinking about how long the cancer had been in my body before the diagnosis and had to ask. The oncologist said it could have been years, but in my case, the cancer was very aggressive and spreading fast, so it was likely only a few months. It made me wonder whether it would have shown up on an X-ray, as my last chest X-ray was on 17th June 2022 and nothing concerning was noted. Not that it would change anything—it was just out of interest.

My fifth chemotherapy

Day 1 – 2nd June

Started my first EC chemo (Epirubicin and Cyclophosphamide), also called the Red Devil. I'd been visualising a smooth experience without side effects. The medication protocol was new—stronger anti-sickness tablets for three days (in a folding "advent calendar" pack), another short-term anti-sickness pill that caused constipation, and my previous milder ones. Steroids were also different: 4 tablets on Day 1, 2 tablets on Days 2 and 3.

I went for a morning run. My brother drove me to the main hospital in Cambridge since this was my first EC round. Usual issues with my veins, but eventually one worked. This chemo is manually injected from a huge syringe—if it spills, it can cause serious damage. Everything went well. Klara picked me up after her work. We got home around 8:30 PM.

Around 10 PM, nausea hit hard. I later realised I had misunderstood the anti-sickness tablet schedule and took them morning and midday instead of morning and evening. That likely made it worse. I called the emergency line and corrected the schedule, then managed to sleep.

Day 2 – 3rd June

Woke up nauseous. Stayed in bed, studied a property investing course. Also explored emotional causes of pulmonary hypertension—realised I might be pushing too hard against life's flow. Began visualising healing for my lungs and heart and committed to doing it daily.

After meds, nausea eased. I helped Mum with lunch and felt well enough to go out. A friend and I went for an 8 km walk. I'd expected steroids to give me the same energy as before—but this time was different.

Past the halfway point, I became very weak. No shortcut back. I made it to her place (7 km total), collapsed into a chair. She gave me fruit and water. After resting, she drove me home.

I realised I'd misjudged my limits—this new chemo affected me differently than the previous rounds.

Day 3 – 4th June

I woke up nauseous, exhausted, and with pressure on my chest and occasional strong heartbeats. I took my meds and tried to study and write but had to lie down again around 11.

During a morning meditation with Angelic Reiki, I asked

for healing of both pulmonary hypertension and cancer, in perfect order, and for insight into any blocks. I had a profound connection with Mother Meera and a healing vision involving Jesus. It was powerful and new.

Lisa, another dear friend, ran a muddy race for a cancer charity in my name today—one of three friends doing this. I felt deeply supported and blessed.

Later, I helped cook lunch and went for a gentle walk with Mum to collect elderflowers for cordial—using Grandma's recipe but without refined sugar.

As it was Sunday, I reflected on the week. I realised I wanted to live more in the present, let go, stop pushing so hard, and allow life to flow. I felt re-energised about my healing and my goals, including financial ones.

That night, sitting with Mum, I had an intense craving—for frankfurters! Despite normally avoiding processed foods, I ate almost four sausages with mustard, and oddly, it helped my nausea. I chose to listen to my body, and it worked.

Day 4 & 5 – 5th & 6th June

I had slept well but woke with chest pressure, noticeable heartbeat, fluid retention, fatigue, nausea, and frequent bowel movements. Day 4, as with previous cycles, was the hardest—but this one wasn't as bad.

I worked the whole day to distract myself, with naps during lunch and after work. The fullness in my stomach persisted, and chest discomfort didn't improve.

Mum brought me a burdock and dandelion drink—less ideal ingredients but it soothed my nausea better than cola.

That evening, I met Klara to plan our property business

and realised I hadn't gone outside at all—something I usually make sure to do, except on Day 4.

The chest tension and elevated heartbeat were concerning. After talking to Mum, we decided I should call the emergency helpline. They assessed the symptoms and arranged a cardiogram via ambulance to check my heart.

The ambulance arrived at 22:30. Both crew members were kind. The lead paramedic did an ECG and asked if I'd been active before cancer. I said yes—he could tell from my heart rate, which was lower than average, typical for runners. The ECG looked fine, but due to my condition, they had to take me to the hospital as a precaution.

I hadn't expected that and struggled to pack. In hindsight, having a pre-packed bag with a note about snacks would've helped.

The ride was uncomfortable—laid backward, every bump was harsh. It was the roughest vehicle I've been in. The trip felt endless, but we arrived. After a short wait, I got my own small room.

They took my blood pressure, then tried drawing blood but struggled. I'd warned them I needed someone experienced—chemo made my veins fragile. It felt like torture at times.

Around 2 AM I was hungry. I had a sandwich and tea, but reading the label, I was shocked by all the processed ingredients. I ate it anyway—more disappointed by the poor food quality than the taste.

The night dragged on with more ECGs, blood tests, X-rays—and constant interruptions. Just as I'd start to sleep, someone would come in. Morning came slowly.

A doctor finally told me all tests were clear—no heart attack, nothing abnormal. One more ECG was ordered.

Emotionally worn down, I broke down crying. I just wanted to be home, eat well, and rest. The doctor was kind and said my feelings were valid—I was young to face this and going through a lot.

After he left, I opened a book Shelly had given me. Her partner had died from cancer near the time of my diagnosis. I hadn't read it until then. I flipped to a random page. The author, an integrative oncologist, wrote that people healed in many ways—natural, conventional, or spiritual—but all shared one thing: belief.

That struck me deeply. I realised I didn't need to doubt my choice. Belief matters most. I believed in my treatment—and everything else I was doing to support my body and mind. That belief would help me heal.

That chapter helped me deal with the fear of damaging my body through chemotherapy. I accepted the fact that this is my journey, and everyone's journey is different. I was still hoping there might be a chance to avoid the operation.

From speaking to doctors and nurses who came into my room, all results seemed to be okay—but the waiting was daunting. After an unexpected night in the hospital, with hardly any sleep, frequent bowel movements, no shower, and no clean clothes, I just didn't feel right in myself. I was becoming very impatient again.

They finally came to tell me that I would be released home once the doctor signed it all off. Which meant another uncertain waiting period, as they were busy with other patients and urgent cases. They asked me to arrange for someone to collect me.

And that's when I broke down again and started crying.

I felt so weak and defeated after that night, that even

simple tasks—which normally wouldn't take more than a blink of an eye—felt like climbing Kilimanjaro.

Even though I had a WhatsApp group set up exactly for situations like this—where I could just send one message and ask if anyone was around to help—I wasn't able to do even that. I had people in the group like Klara, who I think even offered to give me a lift if I needed it, or Ed, who lives just 15 minutes from the hospital.

But I felt paralysed.

I felt so awful—mentally, emotionally, and physically—that I just didn't want anyone to see me. I felt like I looked like I'd just finished two days of partying—and I was stinky. That's how I felt: ashamed.

So I told them I didn't have anyone at that moment who could pick me up.

They suggested public transport, which felt even worse. But I pushed back—not only because of how I felt physically, but also because I didn't want to risk catching anything as a chemo patient. I refused to expose myself to bacteria and viruses on public transport.

The last option they suggested was a taxi. But I felt it was a bit unfair for me to have to pay for a taxi home when I didn't even choose to come to the hospital in the first place. I hadn't wanted to come—and now I was expected to pay for my own way back?

The nurse went away to discuss it with the doctor.

It was getting late in the afternoon, and I got hungry. I was so desperate that I just had a bun with chicken and mayonnaise. First of all, it was really bad food—no nutrition, full of preservatives, meat that I didn't want to eat and didn't enjoy eating, not a single piece of vegetable. The whole experience didn't do me any good mentally, and all I wanted was to magically teleport myself home, have a shower, change my clothes, cuddle my mum and cat, and eat a lot of veg and fruit.

Around 6 PM, a nurse told me to pack—my doctor had approved a taxi home, paid by the hospital. The next ten minutes waiting felt endless. I waited a few more minutes outside, feeling uneasy, until the taxi finally pulled up. As soon as we started moving, I began to cry uncontrollably. For about ten minutes, I couldn't stop. It felt like every emotion from the hospital stay—and likely more—had finally poured out.

I got home around 7 PM and was overwhelmed with relief. I hugged my mum, cuddled my cat, showered, and changed into clean clothes. Mum made fresh juice, and I ate vegetables and fruit—I could feel how depleted I was. We watched TV, and I called the sickness line to take the rest of the week off work. I needed time to recover. I felt this had happened for a reason, though I couldn't yet see it.

Day 6 – 7th June

I woke up feeling better but still tired. I still had loose stool, but it was easier to manage than previous chemo side effects. I decided to try running. At first, I doubted I'd even make it 1 km, but I pushed through and ran 3.3 km. It lifted my mood.

I had a few interviews that day, mostly for practice. I'd already signed a six-month extension to my notice period, staying with my employer until mid-December.

Day 7 – 8th June

I felt great in the morning and drove to Cambridge for a 9:15 plastic surgery appointment. Deep down, I was still hoping I might avoid the operation.

At the clinic, they asked questions and examined my breast. As they explained things, the reality suddenly hit. I had hoped the cancer might just go away. I broke down.

They told me I could have a mastectomy with delayed reconstruction, or with immediate reconstruction. One option was to use an implant, but they didn't recommend it because radiotherapy can affect the implant, making it tight and painful, often requiring another operation months later. Another option was using fat from my abdomen to reconstruct the breast. This would be a longer, more complex operation but wouldn't be affected by radiotherapy.

I mentioned I'd been told I have pulmonary hypertension, and that long surgeries aren't advised. The surgeon agreed but asked if I knew why I had it or whether it could be from chemotherapy. I didn't know. My respiratory appointment was booked for 6th September.

He suggested bringing that appointment forward to understand the CT scan result and help me make an informed decision. It didn't fully register then, but on the way home, I kept thinking about what he said. He had planted a seed.

Later that day, I called to reschedule the respiratory appointment. The specialist nurses didn't see a note from the surgeon but agreed to move it when I insisted. It was changed to 27th July.

After doing some research, I found that pulmonary hypertension can, in rare cases, be a side effect of chemotherapy—so I might not even have it.

Still, I hadn't accepted losing my breast. I put all the brochures and leaflets they gave me to the side. I wasn't ready to look at them yet.

Otherwise, I was very active and productive for the rest of the day and went for a 4.3 km run, which helped me both mentally and physically—especially because I wasn't expecting to be able to run so soon after the hospital stay.

Day 8 – 6th June

It was a nice, warm, sunny day, and we decided to drive to the coast and see what Great Yarmouth is like, as many people I know locally go there. It wasn't the type of coast I like, and if I never went there again, I wouldn't feel like I missed out on anything. But many people do like it.

It's just me thinking that it's very commercial and not as picturesque as I would imagine. But we did have a nice day anyway. We found this restaurant on a cliff with a huge terrace and a glass screen so the wind doesn't get to you. It was pretty cool. We both really enjoyed lunch with a sea view. It had a very holiday-like vibe.

I had chips with my lunch, and as I wasn't used to fried food, I started to feel nauseous in the afternoon—but nothing I couldn't manage.

We had a walk on the coast. I spent quite a while standing on the beach, a little bit sideways from other people, just watching and listening to the sea. It was very soothing, and I felt like I was connected to my true self and to the Universe. It felt like the experience was healing.

Later, we went to play crazy golf again, which we really

enjoyed. It was nice, as there were miniatures of buildings on the crazy golf course. We had great fun.

We set off home later in the afternoon, and as we were approaching our village, the phone rang. It was the claim assessor from the insurance company. He was very nice and apologised that it had taken so long. He contacted me to get clarification on a few points.

As expected, the first question was about the smoking status. I explained that it was very difficult to remember the exact times, but I remembered falling ill and not being able or wanting to smoke, and my boyfriend at the time suggesting I try quitting after not smoking for a few days. So I tried it and bought a non-nicotine vaping pen because it was more of a habit to have something in my hand than anything else. I told him two potential years when this could have happened based on when I was with that boyfriend. Although I knew it was less than five years before signing the insurance contract, I didn't voice it aloud and just waited to hear what he would say.

He then asked why I didn't tell them that I had a mammogram and ultrasound two years before my cancer diagnosis, on the same breast, with a suspicion of some lumps. I felt like he was more concerned about this than the smoking status. The question surprised me, and I was just honest—I said that because they didn't find anything, I completely forgot about it, and it didn't occur to me when filling out the medical questionnaire. I tried to reassure him that it wasn't intentional; it simply didn't cross my mind at that time.

He then thanked me for the information and said he would do the final assessment of the details I provided and let me know on Monday.

I was so nervous. This was the first lump sum of this

kind that I could potentially have in my life—and I wanted to invest it in properties to help us get started. Now I was not only nervous because the non-smoking status wasn't exactly correct, but also because I had forgotten to mention the previous mammogram.

I had signed that I was a non-smoker, but I'm not sure if I had read it properly at the time—it meant being a non-smoker for five years when filling in the form, and that wasn't the case. I only realised that when they asked about it after I submitted the claim.

There was nothing more I could do—only visualise and pray with my whole being.

Days 9 & 10 – 10th & 11th June

I woke up on Saturday feeling well. The nausea had lifted, though I still had loose stool—not quite diarrhoea. I realised both chemo drugs had likely destroyed my gut bacteria. I focused on restoring it with natural, non-dairy probiotics. Despite common belief, most dairy products are too processed to be genuinely beneficial.

It was a beautiful 27-degree day. I went for a run before it got too hot. The rest of the day we spent at home—lunch in the garden, card games with Mum, even taking Max the cat outside on a lead. It was relaxing, sunny, and I finally felt fully recovered from chemo round five.

Sunday followed the same peaceful rhythm. I was preparing myself mentally for Monday's insurance outcome, visualising the money landing in my account—it felt powerful and focused.

Day 11 – 12th June

I started the day with a run, trying to shake off the anxiety around the claim. I began work at 8 and immersed myself in a task. Just after 9 AM, I saw the email from my insurance company—my critical illness claim was approved.

I was overwhelmed with happiness. It felt like my visualisation had worked—I had focused on the outcome, not the process, and it came through. I promised myself I'd apply that same mindset to my healing.

More good news followed. HR called to say that due to a recent policy clarification, I'd still receive 50% of my bonus despite being in a notice period. I hadn't expected that at all.

And then, a message from Klara—she'd entered a Facebook competition, calling me her hero for going through chemo. Her comment won, and we received a box of 20 plant-based, refined sugar–free vegan chocolates—our favourites.

They say good things come in threes, and that day, they did.

Day 12 – 13th June

I felt well and grateful for how quickly I'd bounced back from the chemo. After my run and a day of work, I met up with my work friends for dinner. We sat outside, and for a few hours, everything felt wonderfully normal—as if there were no cancer, no treatments. I got home at 11 PM, which was unheard of for me.

Day 13 – 14th June

I dropped my car off for its MOT and service, picked up a courtesy car, and made it back in time to start work. The car passed, and I retrieved it before an evening meeting with Klara about the property business we'd launched in April.

Day 14 – 15th June

I began with a run that powered me through the day. I still had two interviews, just in case something permanent and supportive came up, though I was leaning toward going freelance in 2024.

Something unexpected happened: a reminder popped up on my phone. I had set it while in Malta, long before the diagnosis. It read: "Wait for the bonus in June, resign, and move to Malta." I reviewed what that would take—getting a job there, moving the cat, building retreats. It was a reminder of an old dream. Life had since shifted in new directions, but the dream was still alive.

Later, I met my new chemo friend from the Outreach Centre. We had coffee in Ely, and she told me her story. Her tumours had shrunk—until she was given the same EC chemo I had just started. After that, her cancer began spreading, and she only found out post-treatment. Her story terrified me. I decided immediately that I would ask for a scan to check my progress as soon as possible.

That same day, I spoke to another friend, had another property meeting with Klara, did some gardening, and even walked Max again. I had no idea how I fit it all in. My feet certainly didn't appreciate it—they were swollen, likely from the chemo.

Day 15 – 16th June

I felt okay but still had swollen feet and ankles. After working in the morning, I drove to an outdoor lunch with colleagues. One of my friends was leaving the company, and it was my first time seeing everyone in person since starting chemo back in March. I was excited—and it felt like a small return to normal life.

That day, I left my mum in Ely, which is something we had started doing so she could browse around the shops, go for a coffee, and enjoy Ely—some time for herself. She loves Ely, so she enjoyed those few hours I left her there whenever I went somewhere else past Ely. It was a nice day, so we walked Max in the garden when we got back.

I had been having a lot of thoughts and anxiety recently about the whole impact of the conventional treatment on my body and was reading a lot about people healing naturally. I was so frustrated—why did I have to heal the conventional way when others heal naturally? I was still trying to find all sorts of reasons why I shouldn't or couldn't do the conventional treatment. I could opt out at any time. But then I was too scared—what if it didn't work? I think my belief system wasn't strong enough to rely on natural healing alone.

I knew that if my diagnosis were terminal, I might go a more adventurous and brave route if there were no conventional treatment to help me—but there was. I started asking for more signs or guidance in my meditations and in my thoughts, especially after the first sign I received from randomly opening a page in the book by the integrative oncologist.

It wasn't just the chemo I was fed up with by then—I didn't want to have my breast removed, as I thought it would make me feel incomplete. And if I went for the operation, I definitely didn't want my lymph nodes to be removed. I had read that it makes it harder for the body to remove toxins and can come with all sorts of side effects.

Suddenly, I received a message from one of the Silva Method instructors who I had never spoken with before. She had seen my messages asking for healing in the group chat and said she normally doesn't engage in the WhatsApp chats, but she felt guided to reach out to me. She said exactly the things I had been searching for, without me even asking. She said that when it comes to cancer, she wouldn't play with fire. She shared her personal experience and advised me on specific mind control techniques and visualisations.

That was the sign I needed to continue with the conventional treatment. I decided to continue, even with the operation, but to program and visualise being able to keep my lymph nodes and be clear of cancer. I was still trying to visualise that I would no longer need the operation, but I didn't have a strong belief in that.

I also discovered a DICCC technique from Marisa Peer, which involves repeating certain affirmation-like statements and instructions for the body. I ordered prayer beads and repeated each statement 108 times, one bead at a time.

Day 16 & 17 – 17th & 18th June

It was Saturday and we took it easy. My feet were still swollen, though less so, and my eyes became a bit irritated—like I had an allergy or something. We spent the day reading, doing little bits and bobs, and I was packing for my trip on Sunday.

My mum was teaching online, so I decided to set off on my first trip and walk on my own since the cancer diagnosis.

Sunday was a nice, hot, sunny day, and I went to one of my favourite places—a National Trust site, Wicken Fen. I chose a slightly different walk, but it was great. I walked over 12 kilometres, which I hadn't done in a very long time.

Thanks to experiences like this, I could feel a sense of normality in an extremely difficult time. I loved it, and it gave me so much new energy and enthusiasm to continue my journey.

Day 18 – 19th June

Amazing day! I received the money from my insurance, felt a huge financial relief first time in my life. And an opportunity to start something new in my life. I didn't want to just spend it, I wanted to invest it and use it to be able to live without a 9-5 job to try to go freelance and set up my own business.

Someone told me about castor oil on my breast healing compress as apparently it reduces tumours. I didn't do much research into it and didn't know if it actually does something. But I did it anyway. The mind is in a strange mode when you have cancer – people either give up or try everything they can to recover. For me it was the latter. And this couldn't hurt.

Day 19 to 21 - 20th to 22th June

Nothing much was happening in these last days of the cycle. I was working, continuing setting up the property business, going for runs, spending time outdoors, trying to cook new recipes and just live a normal life. I continued with my healthy diet, the castor oil compress (just in case it does anything) and the only side effects left were the swollen feet and my eyes got watery and my eyelids swollen a bit. I felt more tired but in a way that I could do everything just had to go to bed early.

My sixth chemotherapy

Day 1 – 23th June

I began the day with meditation, asking for guidance toward treatments that would heal without compromising my quality of life. After a run and a few work meetings, I napped and then headed to chemo session number six—finally! This one was at the local Outreach Centre, just five minutes from home, and it turned out to be the quickest session yet. My 14:30 appointment was finished by 16:00—smooth, simple, and vein access wasn't a problem for once.

Back home, we took Max out in the garden. I took my anti-sickness tablets but couldn't eat—just had fresh carrot juice. I started feeling nauseous and overheated, so my mum cooled me down with a cold towel. By 23:00, I felt really unwell, even though I'd followed all the medication protocols. The effects of this chemo came on faster. I drank lemon water and managed to fall into a deep sleep.

Day 2 – 24th June

Wanting to avoid steroid-induced sleeplessness and the agitated, "wired" feeling they gave me, I stopped taking them the day after chemo. I figured it was better to rest properly for a few days than to be artificially energised and crash later.

I spent the morning researching the upcoming surgery and writing questions for my appointment on 29th June. I felt nauseous until lunchtime but avoided more steroids. Though I was more tired, I felt calmer overall.

Later, I had strong cravings for bread-like foods. Mum and I walked to the shop for pizzas, bread, and chicken goujons—foods far from my ideal diet but sometimes necessary with chemo's effects on taste and appetite. We made the pizzas, though I only ate a slice. What I really craved was simple: bread, butter, chives, and tomatoes.

We did a little gardening—planted new flowers and made lavender cordial, which was a lovely, refreshing addition to water. We also took Max outside again. It's a slow process, mostly standing around, but he loves it.

Despite medication, nausea worsened through the evening. I had some vegetables and a bit more pizza before we moved indoors to rest.

Day 3 – 25th June

I woke up feeling rough and nauseous. I had a small slice of bread with vegan butter and honey, and tried to eat a banana, but ended up sleeping most of the morning. It was disappointing, especially with perfect 31-degree weather outside—my favourite kind of day—but I couldn't do more than rest in bed.

Though I could've taken steroids to feel more active, I chose not to. I asked Mum to bring me a dandelion and burdock fizzy drink. I don't usually drink sugary beverages, but I listened to what my body asked for—and it helped.

For lunch, I managed a bit of pizza with cucumbers and tomatoes, then a slice of bread with butter and honey. Afterward, I went back to sleep for the afternoon.

Later, I realised I had a cardio exam on Monday, and the hospital hadn't given instructions for taking stronger anti-sickness medication after Day 3. I called the advisory line to ask if I could take one more of the strong tablets, as Mondays were always the hardest post-chemo. They approved it but warned against prolonged use due to constipation risks. Still, it gave me some peace of mind.

I was able to sit outside briefly before dinner. Mum made mushroom veggie soup, and I managed to eat some, along with two slices of bread—one with chives, tomato, and pepper, the other with honey—and a banana. My appetite was better this time. I went to bed at 9 PM and slept through the night.

Day 4 – 26th June

I woke feeling less drained than Sunday. I had my usual fresh juice and some bread with butter and honey before heading to the hospital. My friend Ed picked me up—even though it was the opposite direction for him—which I appreciated deeply. He also brought me home afterward.

The heart scan looked good, with less fluid around my heart than before. I took the stronger anti-sickness pill, and although the car ride made me queasy, I didn't get sick.

At home, I had soup, then more bread with butter and honey. I worked in the afternoon and, as usual, had more bread with chives and tomato for dinner.

That evening, I had a spiritual session with Mel. During the healing, I could smell one of her essences even though I hadn't sprayed it. We worked on clearing old anger, envy, and fear of not being loved—healing patterns tied to self-worth and safety. By the end, I felt deeply loved and secure, no matter what was happening.

The nausea returned later, and I went to bed early.

Day 5 – 27th June

I worked all day but still felt tired, nauseous, and skipped breakfast—just had my morning juice. I felt a bit better after lunch and drove to Ely with Mum for a short shop at Waitrose.

Dinner was the usual soup and bread with butter, chives, and tomato. Later, I reviewed and organised my questions for the surgeon and went to bed at 9.

Day 6 – 28th June

I still felt like I had a hangover but slightly improved. I worked but got tired quickly. At one point, my voice changed—it sounded like I'd inhaled helium. Mum laughed, calling me a Smurf.

In the afternoon, I went for a run and managed 2.7 km. It really helped lift my mood. Later, I had a business meeting with Klara. By the end, I was completely exhausted.

This round hit me harder than chemo 5—more nausea, more fatigue, and an overall worse physical toll. Maybe it was because I wasn't in hospital this time or because I didn't take steroids. I felt physically worse but mentally stronger.

I tried going to bed at 10 but couldn't sleep. I got up, had a cookie and tea, and finally slept after 11.

Day 7 - 29th June

That morning I meditated and asked my guides for clarity. I wasn't sure whether to accept another job if one came or focus on new ventures after my notice ends. By mid-morning, I got rejections from every job I'd applied for—including one scheduled for Friday. It felt like a message from the Universe that this wasn't where I needed to focus now—and that I was safe, just as I am.

I worked in the morning and left at 10:30 for my breast clinic appointment. I met with the surgeon and had another ultrasound—the one I requested after my chemo friend's story about her tumours spreading after this drug frightened me.

The consultation went well. I asked every question I'd prepared. It was clear they weren't used to patients being this thorough and wanted to move on quickly, but I didn't let that rush me. This was about my body, and I needed answers.

The surgeon said I might not need radiotherapy, but they wouldn't know until after surgery. If I did, it would rule out immediate reconstruction with an implant. I asked about beam therapy—an experimental alternative my friend mentioned—but they didn't seem familiar with it.

I started to consider using belly fat for reconstruction but wasn't sure if that was possible with suspected pulmonary hypertension. The surgeon confirmed that if the diagnosis stood, that kind of long surgery wouldn't be advised.

Then came the ultrasound. It's always nerve-wracking when they're silent while scanning. I visualised the tumours gone, like I do every day. Then the technician spoke: the smaller tumour had disappeared, all calcifications were gone, and only the one behind the nipple remained—but it was smaller, flatter, and narrower.

Tears filled my eyes. Everything was moving in the right direction.

Looking back at earlier scans: in April, I could no longer feel the second tumour, and the main one had shrunk in density. In May, the second tumour was gone, and the main one was flatter. In June, the breast was clear except for the primary tumour, now down from 44mm to 33mm. I was emotional and uplifted.

Later, I saw my homeopath for a check-in and crystal healing. I always looked forward to those two hours of calm. She was thrilled with my progress, and I felt the healing process had sped up since starting the remedies. During the session, I had visions—of a baby, of relationships, of my deep connection to the Divine, and even dolphins. My healer asked if I connected with fairies, which hadn't crossed my mind—but maybe she sensed something.

By the end, I felt lighter, more centred—like the chemo's weight had lifted.

Day 8 to 10 - 30th June to 2nd July

I woke up feeling better, but by evening, I felt off again. It was that same heavy nausea I'd once blamed on greasy food. Now I knew it was a chemo side effect. I had loose stool and barely ate. Though I usually review and reflect on the last day of the month, I couldn't finish. I just didn't feel well.

The next day, I felt much better and finished my monthly reflection before going for a run. At first, I was disappointed—I hadn't made much progress on my blog or YouTube. But then I remembered: I'd started a business, worked full-time, and was recovering from chemo. Two sessions had fallen in June. I had to give myself credit.

Most importantly, my health had improved dramatically—the fastest yet. I'd also noticed a lot of spiritual signs. Random answers to my questions would show up in surprising ways. Emotionally, I was focusing on clearing anger, reclaiming my power, and healing old disbelief. Spiritually, it felt like something deep was shifting.

We met my brother, his wife, and my nephew in Ely around 11 AM, sitting on a terrace by the river. It was a beautiful day that felt wonderfully normal again. They were happy to hear about my healing progress. On the way back, we picked up a wardrobe catalogue—I'd been putting off adding a fitted door to my room for two years.

I felt full the rest of the day and didn't eat again. We took it easy, watching our favourite series.

We kept Sunday relaxed. I wrote a bit of a business plan and tried a new recipe for lunch. Inspired, I made a pickled vegan camembert. I went running in the afternoon, then rested with some TV. I felt less bloated and ate a bit for dinner. Two new symptoms appeared: mouth ulcers and thinning eyebrows.

Day 11 to 15 – 3rd to 7th July

On Monday, I went for a morning run before work. A will specialist visited to help me start planning—it was time. I wasn't expecting to die, but cancer had brought the topic closer. I wanted to ensure everything would be smooth for my loved ones if anything happened.

We had our regular business meeting, and for the first time this cycle, I felt hungry in the evening and ate dinner.

Tuesday began with another morning run. I worked all day, then met my chemo friend for coffee and a walk, making it back in time for the Silva Graduate group. That community always lifts me—it keeps my mind on healing and positivity instead of illness.

During meditation and visualisation over the next couple of days, I saw a fairy healing my breast, ulcers, and cold sore. It reminded me of my healer's question about fairies, and how I'd recently pulled out my dolphin and fairy oracle deck from Czechia. It all started to make sense—I was more connected than I'd realised. I also felt a deep connection with dolphins.

To me, it didn't matter what form the vision took—what mattered was focusing on healing and the end result.

I went for a walk through the village, stopped at my "recharging field," and picked up fruit and veg from a roadside stall.

In my next meditation, the fairy appeared again, healing my lungs, lymphatic system, and vessels. It was a beautiful start to the day. I ran 5 km, worked all day, and felt much better—the ulcers and cold sore were also improving.

On Friday, I had nice plans and no more ulcer. I went for a run, then met my friend Becky for a walk and lunch. It gave me that feeling of normal life again—beautiful weather, lovely company.

Day 16 & 17 – 8th & 9th July

Saturday began with a 6 km run. As usual, I forgot it was Parkrun day and ended up running against the crowd—always funny. I met Ellie in Ely for lunch and a riverside walk. We ended up in a little chocolate shop, and I had a few dairy chocolates—breaking from my usual diet, but it felt okay.

Back home, we installed new crystal lamps in my room and booked my mum's flight home, as chemo was nearly over. We ended the evening with a lazy telly night.

By Sunday, I was three days into socialising. I didn't do much in the morning apart from a 5 km run to boost my energy. I felt okay, though one ear was blocked.

Klara invited us for lunch—she made a healthy version of strawberry dumplings with poppy seeds, vegan butter, and coconut yogurt. My brother and nephew came by later, and we walked to the local playground.

In a burst of energy, I started baking mini vegan chocolate tarts with coconut oil and almond butter—but didn't have the energy to finish. We crashed on the sofa with a light dinner and more telly.

Day 18 & 19 – 10th & 11th July

Monday was a typical day—work, an afternoon run, and some planning for the property business. I also went for blood tests before my next chemo. My energy had been lower, and running felt harder, so I asked for iron levels to be checked. They agreed to run iron studies too.

What made the day special was Mum cooking a healthy version of Svíčkova, a traditional Czech meal. It's usually served with beef, but we skipped the meat. It was delicious and brought back childhood memories, especially with a spoonful of cranberry jam. I also finished the tarts I'd started the day before.

Tuesday was uneventful. I worked, and someone came by to show me wardrobe wood options for a quote. We relaxed for the rest of the day.

Day 20 – 12th July

I took Wednesday off to enjoy a nice day before chemo hit again. We drove to London—I wanted to avoid the underground for hygiene reasons and to spare Mum's knee. Parking took some effort, but we found a spot near our destination.

We had lunch at Deliciously Ella's kitchen, one of my favourite brands since changing my diet. It's not organic but uses natural ingredients and fruit sugars. The founder started it due to her own health issues, and the restaurant was fantastic.

After lunch, we browsed perfume shops. I've been planning to replace synthetic perfumes with natural ones. One shop stood out, and I bought two perfumes—plus one for Mum. The scents were beautiful.

Later, we took a black cab to Little Venice for a boat ride to Camden and back. It was charming and relaxing. We left London around 7:30 PM after a quick Waitrose stop.

That evening, I got my blood test results—my iron levels had dropped significantly. I had been right; I really do know my body.

Day 21 – 13th July

Thursday morning, I had an appointment with the plastic surgeon. Sandra came with me. The surgeon asked if I'd considered which surgery I wanted. I mentioned the DIEP tummy flap, but said I'd been told I couldn't have it due to pulmonary hypertension from my CT scan. I was still waiting on a respiratory team review.

He looked surprised and told me, "You don't have pulmonary hypertension—the cardiologist confirmed that in early June." He showed me the note in the system.

I was shocked. No one had told me. It was upsetting, especially after thinking I had a lifelong condition. It reminded me why I stay so involved in my care—because sometimes, critical information falls through the cracks.

But it was incredible news. I'd been visualising healthy lungs and heart daily, and now I was told I didn't have the condition after all. I hadn't focused on how it would happen—just believed it would.

Strangely, I now see the benefit of being taken to hospital by ambulance in June. Without that, I wouldn't have this information now.

We agreed to explore the tummy flap option—a 9-hour surgery, with the first part being mastectomy and the second, reconstructing the breast using fat and blood vessels from my stomach. It's incredible what's possible. I was booked for more tests to ensure my vessels were strong enough. There was a small risk they might not work and I'd be left with only the mastectomy, but most cases go smoothly.

I also had a check-in with oncology and questioned a chemo appointment scheduled for 4th August. They said it was likely a system error but left it in case surgery happened more than six weeks after my last chemo—in which case I'd receive the Phesgo injection.

I also asked for an iron infusion and received an appointment for Tuesday, 18th July. It wasn't ideal, as that would be Day 5 after chemo, when I typically don't feel well enough to drive. I wasn't happy about the timing, but it was the best they could offer at that moment.

My seventh and last chemotherapy

Day 1 – 14th July

I woke up in the morning so excited. I opened my journal and wrote: "The last chemo in my life" and "I love myself." According to the various resources I read, the possible spiritual and emotional causes of cancer could be lined to lack of self-love. I've learned that there could be a part of the patient that doesn't love themselves—or even hates themselves for something—that eats them away. And in many ways, my cancer journey has been about discovering how to love myself more.

I felt very spiritually connected that morning, like I was standing at the beginning of a new chapter in my life.

I went for a run in the morning and then started preparing for a quick trip to Cambridge. I had an appointment with the Chinese herbalist. She sorted out my herbal medicine for the next few weeks and told me to come back after the operation. It had helped me with the side effects of chemotherapy, but I no longer felt drawn to it, so I decided to discontinue it.

I dropped my mum off in Ely on the way so she could browse around the shops. After my appointment in Cambridge, I met up with her again in Ely for lunch at a very authentic riverside tearoom.

Later, I dropped my mum and the car off at home and walked to the outreach centre for my final chemotherapy session.

Unfortunately, it turned out to be a dreadful process. Over an hour passed, and they still couldn't find a vein. It was more challenging than ever before. My veins had become very disrupted, and it was too risky to administer this type of chemo—if it got outside the veins, it could cause major damage, potentially requiring plastic surgery.

They had to reschedule my appointment and managed to book me in the next morning at Cambridge Hospital. I immediately asked if they could give me the iron infusion at the same time as the chemo, so I wouldn't have to come back on Tuesday when I'd be feeling rough. The nurses were amazing—probably feeling sorry that they couldn't go ahead with my last chemo—and they arranged for both treatments to take place the very next day.

They promised I'd be taken care of by Raquel, who is known for having "X-ray vision" when it comes to finding veins.

That evening, I felt physically strange, having already taken steroids and other medication in preparation for the appointment. I still needed to sort out transport to and from the hospital the next morning, so I posted on my WhatsApp group and on Facebook. One of my friends messaged me to offer a lift.

Day 1 – 15th July

After yesterday's unsuccessful attempt, I woke up excited about finally getting my last chemo done—and receiving my iron infusion at the same time. It worked out well in that respect.

My friend Ellie took me to Cambridge for 10 AM. When I arrived at reception, Raquel was already there waiting for me.

She smiled and waved, saying, "I am here, Veronika, waiting for you." Raquel is the nurse known for being able to find and access any vein. She was also the nurse who administered my very first chemotherapy. I was relieved to see her.

I had brought my hot water bottle to help my veins appear more easily. I'd been using it on the way to the hospital, doing everything I could to support the process. This time, I didn't bring my small water bottle—I brought the huge one I use for cold winter nights, over a metre long. I just wanted this final chemo done and dusted.

In the end, Raquel got the vein on her first try. She began administering the chemo around 10:30, and continued with the iron infusion straight afterward. We had a nice chat while she worked. I remember how surprised she was when she noticed I still had some eyelashes—though not many.

By 12:45, I was sitting in my friend's car. I was home by 1:45 PM, just in time for lunch. I fell asleep before 3 PM. I moved to my "after-chemo diet," starting with a small carrot juice and a baguette with vegan butter, chives, and tomato—then another with jam and two mini cheeses for dinner. Later, I had two decaf black teas with honey.

I felt tired and slightly "stoned" from the steroids I had taken and been given, which also explained why I ate more or less normal portions. We watched a film, and I went to bed around 10 PM and slept well.

Day 2 – 16th July

I woke up feeling tired but relatively okay. I continued writing our property business plan in the morning. I began to feel chemo cravings, and I really wanted schnitzel with mashed potatoes. It was the first time I'd craved something like that so soon after a chemo treatment.

I took the car and drove to the international shop and stall in our village. My mum cooked turkey schnitzel and mashed potatoes using plant-based milk, so I still stuck to my dietary choices with that part of the meal. I truly enjoyed it—I love that combination. It reminds me of my childhood.

I had a nap in the afternoon as I was starting to feel nauseous, tired, overheated, and had a very dry mouth. Later, we just watched telly, and I was back in bed around 10 PM.

Day 3 – 17th July

I woke up feeling really unwell. My anti-sickness medication and steroid schedule were out of sync, since my treatment was originally meant to happen on Friday but was pushed to Saturday. So the whole tablet timing was off.

The day was hell. I was extremely weak, felt pressure on my chest, and was very nauseous. I had to sign off from work and spent the whole day lying in bed, feeling sick. I tried to settle my stomach with a plain breakfast—tea, a crumpet, and honey.

For lunch, I managed to eat half of a schnitzel with a spoonful of mashed potatoes and some grated cucumber. Then I went straight back to bed. Later, I woke up with a headache, on top of everything else.

I was craving ice cream, so I had an Ice lolly, as I didn't have any healthier alternative available. I felt worse as the day went on—alternating suddenly between feeling cold and hot. The pressure on my chest increased. I had back pain, neck pain, and needed to use the toilet frequently.

I tried eating a banana and later had some liquid from a cabbage soup for dinner, but couldn't really eat it. I stuck to drinking mineral water. It wasn't until 10 PM that I was able to eat a bowl of veggie broth and take another dose of anti-sickness medication.

This felt like the worst day of the entire chemotherapy course.

Day 4 – 18th July

I slept well but woke tired. The pressure on my chest had eased, but I took the day off to recover. I had a crumpet with vegan butter and honey, black decaf tea, and a few naps. Despite it being only Day 4 post-chemo, I pushed myself to run. After 3.8 km of slow jogging, I felt better. I ate a light lunch with some vegetables.

In the afternoon, a former colleague visited. I was glad to see him but still felt I wasn't quite myself. I napped again after he left. For dinner, I had veggie broth and pickled cabbage, which helped ease the bloated feeling. I joined the Silva group in the evening, felt uplifted, and went to bed by 9 PM.

Day 5 to 8 – 19th to 22nd July

I woke still nauseous on Day 5 but skipped meds. I took another day off and ran 4 km—it helped physically and mentally. Running and driving again always signal to me that I'm turning the corner.

My voice was odd, sound sensitivity lingered, and my blocked ear persisted. I ate plain vegetables, a few mini cheeses, and in the afternoon managed some light gardening, a short walk with Max, and a trip to the local stall for corn. Dinner was veggie broth and corn on the cob. I was in bed again by 9.

Day 6 started with a run, and I decided to work. By the end of the day, I was too tired to drive to Ely for a family visit and had to cancel. I spent the evening resting on the sofa and went to bed around 10 PM.

On Day 7, I felt much better. I had a CT scan to assess if they could use my tummy fat for breast reconstruction. They needed to inject dye into my veins—but accessing a vein was a nightmare. It was painful and stressful, and after the test, the site started bleeding again, requiring a new dressing.

The day was saved by lunch with Mum at a charming Thai restaurant—my first full meal since chemo 7. We did a bit of shopping afterward, and I went for an evening run. I joined the Silva healing session, ending the day calm and grounded.

Day 8 was slow and restful. I ran 4.5 km but otherwise took it easy, knowing Mum was leaving the next day. I craved pickled cabbage again—it really helped my digestion. My ear was still blocked.

Day 9 – 23rd July

My mum flew home after 5.5 months. It felt strange—I'd grown used to her being there, and I knew the house would feel empty. On the way to the airport, she got a delay notice, so we stopped in a nearby town. We found a small café serving the best chai latte I'd ever had—made from real spices, not syrup. It was a special moment.

After dropping her at Luton, I met a friend at a pub near Cambridge. We had a lovely lunch and catch-up, then I drove home. I went for a run later but only had a light dinner.

I felt proud—both of myself and my mum. We had made it through all seven cycles of chemo. And I was finally recovering from the last one.

Day 10 – 24h July

On Monday, I went for a 7 km run before starting work. During the day, I noticed the shower coming loose in my bathroom. Concerned, especially since I was heading to Bournemouth for a few days, I called a plumber who fortunately came within an hour and fixed it.

After work, I packed and left for Bournemouth around 6 PM. I arrived at 10 PM, just as my friend finished work. It was heartwarming to reunite after years—we're both from the same city in Czechia. We stayed up chatting until midnight in her beachside apartment.

Day 11 – 25th July

I woke up to a beautiful sea view. My friend and I visited stunning cliffs and later walked along the beach, visited an upside-down museum, and explored the town centre. We walked 27 km and took 37,000 steps. Exhausted but happy, we relaxed on her balcony before bed.

Day 12 – 26th July

We went for a 7.5 km beach run, followed by lunch at a seaside restaurant. I had vegan fish and chips—deep-fried banana blossoms—which were surprisingly good, though heavy. After lunch, I drove home and arrived around 6–7 PM. My blocked ear still hadn't improved.

Day 13 – 27th July

I ran 4 km and returned to work. Later, I had a long-awaited appointment with the respiratory team to discuss possible pulmonary hypertension. I came prepared with questions, including whether chemo or tumour pressure could cause the condition, and noted inconsistencies between doctors' interpretations of my scans. The oncologist registrar believed early signs were present in my first CT, while my primary oncologist disagreed, leading to growing mistrust.

I also wanted to discuss alternative approaches before committing to lifelong medication, especially given my positive cancer treatment results. I believed I could manage the condition naturally, at least initially. The cardiologist had also noted that pulmonary hypertension was unlikely, giving me hope.

At the appointment, the doctor began by asking why I suspected the condition, so I shared my full story.

The doctor asked many questions, including how active I was. When I mentioned running 4–5 km during chemotherapy, she was visibly surprised. She said this level of activity essentially ruled out pulmonary hypertension, which typically leaves patients breathless even while walking. She explained that CT scans aren't used for diagnosis and confirmed that previous hospital cardiology tests already ruled it out. The team was puzzled as to why I'd been told otherwise.

I left the appointment feeling relieved and happy.

With chemo almost over, I felt a strong need to get

away—to clear my mind and recover emotionally. I had fallen in love with Malta and decided to go there for a few days, followed by a short trip to see family in Slovakia. The cancer experience deepened my appreciation for loved ones and meaningful time together. Oncology gave me the all-clear to travel 2–3 weeks post-chemo—this felt like the right move to recharge for the surgery ahead.

Days 14 to 16 – 28th to 30th July

These days were fairly routine. I continued running and staying active, though I often felt full in the afternoons and could barely eat or drink. My ear was still blocked. I went for a peaceful run at my favourite National Trust site and worked on our property business—finalising the website and completing the business plan.

I also booked my trip: Malta from 6th August and Slovakia from the 9th to the 11th. I was excited, though slightly anxious about leaving my cat, who had grown used to my constant presence—so I kept the trip short.

Day 17 – 31st July

Monday brought an appointment at the breast clinic for a mammogram and ultrasound. I had been visualising cancer-free results, still hoping to avoid surgery, despite knowing how unlikely that was.

With pulmonary hypertension ruled out, all surgical options were now open. I leaned toward reconstruction using tummy fat—it's natural-looking, doesn't require maintenance like implants, and, amusingly, fulfilled my old 2023 goal of losing belly fat, albeit in a way I never expected. Life has a strange way of granting wishes.

Though this method meant a longer recovery, it offered long-term peace of mind. We discussed the possibility of reconstructing both breasts, but due to limited abdominal fat, doing both would require an implant. Since there was no medical necessity for a double procedure, I chose to do one breast for now, keeping future options open.

I expressed concerns to my surgeon about lymph node removal, worrying it would interfere with my body's detoxification. Based on my progress, he proposed a sentinel lymph node biopsy instead. This involves injecting dye the day before surgery to identify the nodes most likely to carry cancer, allowing removal of only a few. This reduces the risk of lymphoedema to 5%, compared to 20% with standard removal. If more extensive removal became necessary, we would proceed, but I planned to support my body through a clean lifestyle. I also requested a plant-based diet during my hospital stay.

Later, I had a scan. The radiologist was pleased to report that the tumour had shrunk compared to the previous scan. I should have felt excited, but I was disappointed—it hadn't disappeared completely. Although I knew that stability or shrinkage was good, emotionally I struggled. Negative thoughts took over, and I felt disheartened.

Day 18 – 1st August

To support my healing, I decided to do a juice fast in line with the full moon, believing it could amplify the benefits. Being the start of a new month, I reflected on July and felt proud of completing chemotherapy and overcoming many challenges. I sensed I was undergoing a major transformation. Though I still felt a void in my love life, I understood I might not have met anyone yet because of the personal changes I was going through.

Still, I couldn't shake the disappointment about the tumour not disappearing. I wasn't questioning the need for surgery—it was more about fear: fear of how I'd feel, how I'd look, and the reality of having a mastectomy.

Day 19 & 20 – 2nd & 3rd August

I received the date of my operation. The anxiety hit hard, and I still hadn't fully processed my emotions from the earlier scan. It felt ungrateful, but it was honest. I'd never had surgery before and was still secretly hoping I could avoid it. But I understood the doctors would always recommend surgery to prevent recurrence. If I had refused it, I would have had to fully own that choice and its consequences.

Even though the tumour had shrunk by 3 mm, I dismissed it as "only 3 mm," even though that was a success. I realised I had been hoping for a miracle, and now I just needed time to accept the reality.

In parallel, I was working on my Employment Tribunal case. I researched no-win, no-fee legal support and discovered through a solicitor's website that I might have legal cover via my home insurance. I checked and found a £150,000 family legal protection clause. I contacted a solicitor I'd already spoken to and arranged for them to be instructed via the insurance. If the claim was denied, we would revert to no-win, no-fee. This took a huge weight off my shoulders.

I also searched for travel insurance, which was tricky with a cancer diagnosis. One company quoted £600 for a six-night European trip. I expected to pay more, but not that much, so I spent hours trying to find a better deal.

I was eventually recommended a travel insurance provider for cancer patients, which sounded promising. But when I told them my cancer hadn't spread, they said they couldn't insure me—ironically, they only covered terminal cases. It made no sense to me, though the representative was kind and advised me to bring my European Health Insurance Card.

The high insurance cost stemmed from three factors: the cancer hadn't been surgically removed, I hadn't completed all treatments, and was still mid-process. They told me that once treatment was complete, the price would drop from £600 to under £200. I ultimately secured a policy for £250—still expensive, but manageable. Without the health condition, I might have risked travelling uninsured.

I contacted breast care nurses with a few follow-up questions. I asked whether I could swim in the sea after finishing chemo on 4th August, and was told the risk of infection would be much lower, so it was fine. I also asked about the Zoladex injections I'd originally been told I'd need every 4 weeks. They clarified I didn't need them after all, since my cancer wasn't oestrogen-driven—meaning my periods might return naturally.

Wanting more control over my health, I requested a full blood test to check for any vitamin or mineral deficiencies. While blood was taken, the results only covered vitamin D, B12, and some routine markers. The oncologist registrar didn't understand the nature of my request and sent me for repeat testing unnecessarily. When she called back, it was difficult to explain what I was after. She claimed they don't do full nutrient panels because results take six months and deficiencies would be felt physically. When I asked if I should go private, she said it would be a waste of money.

This was the same registrar who previously told me—incorrectly—that I had pulmonary hypertension, needed Zoladex, and that signs had already shown in a March CT. Her inconsistent and unreliable advice made me distrust her further.

In the end, my vitamin D and B12 levels were above mid-range—unsurprising, as I was drinking three fresh organic juices a day. I decided to let it go and trust my body, especially now that chemo was complete.

Physically, I noticed changes: a toenail lifting with a blister, swelling in my legs, and puffy eyes. Mentally, I was still struggling—the scan results, insurance ordeal, and the reality of surgery were overwhelming.

Still, this marked a huge milestone: the final day of my seventh chemotherapy cycle. I had completed it. I survived it. And even though I didn't feel celebratory, it was an accomplishment.

Day 21 – 4th August

I went for my first haircut since before chemo. I hadn't shaved my head completely and had a few random strands left. It looked odd, but I'd left them to observe the process. Now, with hair regrowth expected, I got them trimmed so everything could grow evenly.

Later that afternoon, I had a pre-op consultation with my plastic surgeon—on the same day I marked the end of my final chemo cycle. After the respiratory team cleared me, I opted for the longer procedure: a mastectomy with immediate reconstruction using a tummy flap.

The plan was to remove all tissue from my right breast, then take fat and blood vessels from my tummy—confirmed as suitable during the CT scan—and transfer them to form a new breast. The skin would be preserved, giving it a natural look. Though there were risks, it felt like the right choice for me. An added bonus: I'd finally have a flat tummy.

They assessed my blood vessels using a method similar to cardiac auscultation. The vessels on the right side were deemed viable. They explained the reconstruction like plumbing—disconnecting the vessels in my tummy, transferring them with fat to the breast, and reconnecting them there. Keeping the area warm post-surgery was crucial to ensure the vessels stayed alive; otherwise, the reconstruction would fail.

The surgery was scheduled for 25th August, and I'd already coordinated with my mum to arrive before then. She could only stay a limited time due to UK immigration rules (max 180 days per year), so her timing needed to be precise to support me post-op.

However, I was told there would likely be a strike on 25th August, and the surgery might be postponed. The outcome would only be confirmed the morning of the operation. The uncertainty hit me hard—I'd been feeling low all week, and this pushed me over the edge. My mum doesn't speak English and wasn't comfortable navigating alone, which added to the stress. I broke down in tears during the appointment.

The surgeon, though blunt, reassured me that my mum would be more useful after I was discharged, not while I was in the hospital. I normally take pride in organising everything myself, but at that moment, I felt overwhelmed and powerless.

Later, I saw that I had overreacted. Any surgery can be postponed. It was wiser to arrange for my mum to arrive after the operation and find someone to help her with travel. Still, the immigration limitations were frustrating—we couldn't easily extend her stay without applying for a complex and costly visa.

Despite seeing a logical way forward, I still felt emotionally exhausted. The entire week had been heavy.

VI

Between Chemotherapy and Operation

5th August

It was Saturday, and I started packing for my trip, though I wasn't in a good mental space. The week had begun with a scan showing my tumour had shrunk another 3 mm, but some cancer remained. I had been hoping to be cancer-free before surgery, and this was my last scan before the operation.

Alongside that, the travel insurance hassle and the Employment Tribunal stress weighed on me—though discovering my home insurance included legal cover was a relief. On top of it all, I noticed a blister lifting one of my toenails and panicked that it might prevent me from travelling.

I called the cancer support line, sent a photo, and the nurse confirmed I could go—so long as I avoided infection, pools, and the sea. That was disappointing but manageable. I packed and took the rest of the day slowly. By evening, I felt a bit better.

6th August

I left for the airport at 4 AM in 10°C weather—harsh for someone who thrives in warmth. I had porridge at the airport, then flew to Malta. After landing, I picked up a rental car, changed clothes, and went straight to a plant-based restaurant. Just hours after leaving cold England, I was enjoying lunch in 27°C sunshine by the sea. It felt like coming home—like nothing bad had happened.

Afterwards, I visited another bay, had a juice, browsed shops, picked up fruit and water from a supermarket, and continued along the coast toward my hotel. I stopped at the Mediterraneo Marine Park to ask if I could swim with dolphins—a lifelong dream. Online bookings were full, but they had a cancellation the next day at 11 AM, so I booked it. Although it meant entering a pool, which the nurse had advised against, I was determined to make it happen.

I also stopped to visit a coastal tower before finally reaching my hotel. After a bit of trouble parking, I checked in and was pleasantly surprised—modern room, large terrace, sea view, and a rooftop infinity pool (though too windy to use that day).

That evening, I went to the Café Del Mar closing party. I didn't mind going alone—I was determined to embrace life after 5.5 months of chemo. I danced for two hours, even if the music wasn't fully my style, and left at 10 PM, exhausted after being up since 3:30 AM.

Back at the hotel, a black and white cat was sitting right on the front carpet. As a cat lover, it reminded me of my own cat Max, who was likely waiting by the window, wondering where I had gone.

I had an amazing day and felt like a completely different person already.

7th August

I went for a run along the beach first thing in the morning and then stopped at a pharmacy to look for something to protect my toe. I found these plastic finger protectors that I managed to put on my toe and wrap around so that it stayed protected. Awesome!

Then I set off to the Mediterraneo Park. We had to put on neoprene suits, which is something I hadn't done before. It was very difficult to put on, but I did it and joined the group. The instructor looked at me and said, "You have it the other way round." Oh no! That was a nightmare! It took me a while, but I finally got it right.

I had to wear a headscarf because of my bald head and the direct sun, to protect myself from sunburn. There were signs saying no head coverings were allowed, but in the end, they let me wear it when I explained why.

Okay—so now I was ready: headscarf on, toe wrapped and protected, and neoprene the correct way round—to go and meet a dolphin.

We were told the dolphin was deaf and wouldn't survive in the wild. That made me feel much better about the whole captivity aspect, because they were taking care of him instead.

We stood in a row, and the dolphin arrived. His name was Nino. He greeted each person individually. I was last. He came to me, greeted me—and splashed me in the face. He didn't splash anyone else. It felt like a sign from the Universe.

I started crying—not because he splashed me, but because

I suddenly felt so connected to the dolphin energy. It was a different kind of cry—I cried from the bottom of my heart. It was something extraordinary that I had never felt before. I felt love, forgiveness, and a huge emotional release. It was like something shifted and healed.

I suddenly felt the happiest I had ever been in my life.

I drove to Mista, ate at a plant-based restaurant, browsed shops, and then headed to Golden Bay—but it was too crowded. I found a quieter beach nearby and decided to swim in the sea despite the nurse's advice, using a makeshift toe wrap for protection. I felt it was worth it to enjoy Malta fully.

That evening, I walked along the beach and sat on a rock, watching the sea. It felt like the trauma of the past months was washing away—physically, emotionally, mentally, and spiritually. I felt deeply at peace.

8th August

I went for a morning beach run, then visited the Blue Grotto caves and took a boat trip. Afterwards, I had lunch inland, then returned to the Blue Grotto viewpoint. There I met a Scottish man also headed to the airport, so I gave him a lift.

That evening, I flew to Slovakia to visit my family. Despite a delayed flight, I was overwhelmed with emotion seeing my dad for the first time in four years—after the pandemic and everything I'd been through. I cried when we reunited.

9th & 10th August

I spent these days with my family—my parents, uncle, aunt, cousin, and her family. It was a joyful time. Cancer had made me realise how important they are to me, and that I want to prioritise seeing them more often.

Physically, my toe was still holding up, though two smaller toenails were loose. My eyebrows began to regrow, which felt more significant than my hair loss—my face had looked so unfamiliar without them.

I also found an old notebook with a prayer to Archangel Michael from 2002. It reminded me how protected I've always been. I reconnected with the state of spiritual flow I'd felt in the past—when creativity and purpose align. I realised that everything I'd studied—mind control, Reiki, mental programming—was meant to help others now, especially women with breast cancer.

11th August

I went for a run, had lunch with my mum and uncle for her birthday, then spent the afternoon with my parents before flying home. I left feeling deeply fulfilled. I had visited Malta—my soul place—swum with dolphins, reunited with my dad, and experienced beautiful moments with my family. I felt protected and spiritually connected.

12th to 23rd August

Back home, I returned to my routine briefly before signing off from work to prepare for surgery. I began organising what to pack for the hospital, shopping for post-surgery bras and pants, and planning how I'd spend recovery time when my activity would be limited.

I was still dealing with physical side effects: swollen ankles, chemo-damaged toenails (some loose, some hard and uncuttable), and blocked ears. I had requested an ENT appointment but hadn't heard back. Despite these frustrations, I kept moving forward.

And for the first time—I noticed hair starting to grow back.

In the days leading up to the operation, I focused on self-care. I went on long walks, sunbathed, and did things that made me feel connected and calm. I felt spiritually aligned—with myself, the Universe, and the angels.

In the days leading up to the operation, I felt a deep connection to the spiritual world. It reminded me of the time before my final diagnosis—when I was waiting to learn if the cancer was curable. This time, I didn't feel close to death, but deeply connected and safe.

Through meditation, I experienced profound forgiveness and emotional clearing. I felt unity, love for others, and self-compassion. On 20 August, I wrote in my journal that I was ready to be held by my spiritual guides and angels as I went under anaesthesia. I was at peace with any outcome, even the possibility of not waking up—though I also felt that if I returned, it would be to live a new life, aligned with purpose.

Walks in nature kept my spirit high. I entered a calm, almost zen-like state, deeply connected to Source. I began programming my mind for a successful operation, visualising a smooth procedure, perfect reconstruction, and a joyful hospital stay. I imagined feeling content, even away from home—which is hard for me, since I deeply value being with my cat Max and my own space.

Reflecting on the journey, I realised how cancer had changed me. I learned to care for my body better—not just through nutrition and detox but in small ways like skincare and nail care. I started loving my body more. I also learned that asking for help is okay, and that even in the darkest times, I could create joy and beautiful memories.

The trip between chemo and surgery helped reset my entire being—physically, emotionally, and spiritually. It brought clarity, balance, and strength for what was next. It reminded me of my passion to help others and reaffirmed my belief in mind-body techniques like the Silva Method, Reiki, and visualisation. These tools, along with prayer, had led to incredible empowerment during this difficult time.

Though the tumour hadn't disappeared completely by the 31 July scan, I came to peace with the idea that surgery was part of my journey—perhaps necessary so I could truly understand and help other women facing breast cancer. I felt guided and supported by God, the Universe, and the Angels throughout.

24th August

The day before surgery, I had a hospital appointment with the plastic surgeon. He marked up my body with notes like "MX" (mastectomy) and "SLB" (sentinel lymph node biopsy). It was a hot summer day, and I wore a strappy top, so the markings were visible—but I didn't care.

I walked through Cambridge to my favourite restaurant, had a beautiful lunch, and treated myself to a vegan caramel tiramisu. I enjoyed the moment fully, unaffected by what others might think of my marker-covered skin. I was living in acceptance, presence, and peace.

Later in the afternoon, I had another appointment for the sentinel lymph node biopsy preparation. They injected a very weak radioactive liquid into my breast. It was stingy—but nothing compared to biopsies! It stung for maybe two or three minutes, and then nothing. They said it would create a blister, but they put a plaster on and told me to keep it on for the following day.

The dye helps highlight the lymph nodes that would have been affected first if the cancer had already spread at the time of the original diagnosis.

It was a long day—one appointment at 10:45 and another at 15:15, with a half-hour delay. By the end, I just wanted to get out of the car park. I needed my parking ticket to go through a machine so I could pay the discounted rate. There was a lady taking her time fiddling with something, and I gently asked if they could run my ticket through quickly at the same time. The guy replied, "I'm still serving a customer," and I said, "I know, but it's been a hard day and I have to be back for major surgery at 7 AM."

She walked away anyway. But then, as I passed by her car, she was very rude and shouted at me. She swore at me and called me a selfish b*tch. That hit me hard. After everything I had been through and what was still ahead of me, it felt so unfair. I felt awful.

But it turned out to be another blessing—because she made me cry. I cried almost the whole way home, and I needed that. I felt like I hadn't had a proper meltdown yet, and it felt so good. Like some stuck emotions were finally released.

Later, I packed for the hospital and arranged everything for my mum's arrival. We agreed that once I'd had the operation, she would fly over. We bought her a flexible ticket, so my friend could help her change it if needed, and my friend was also picking her up at the airport. I knew everything was sorted, and that gave me peace of mind.

What I didn't realise when coming to the appointment was not to wear anything light-coloured—because of the markings. I hadn't noticed anything they drew on me during previous appointments. But this time, I wore salmon-coloured shorts and a light pink bra. I had to wear paper hand towels underneath, but the pen still got on my clothes. Thankfully, I managed to use a special stain removal product, and the shorts were saved. The bra still had a bit of pen on it.

VII

Operation & Recovery

Operation & 1st week of recovery

25th August – The Day of the Operation

My friend picked me up at 6:30 and dropped me off at the hospital around 7 AM. I was admitted very quickly and placed in a waiting area with my own bed. Time went by fairly quickly.

I had to provide a urine sample in the morning for further checks, and I met my whole team for the day, including the anaesthesiologist. They all started coming in around 8 AM to say hello, which was really nice. I met my whole power team. I was also surprised to learn that I would have two plastic surgeons performing the operation.

I was very anxious. It was my first operation, and I shared my concerns with the surgeons. I spoke about my fear of letting go of control and the fear of pain. They explained to me that they would send me into a beautiful sleep and that I'd be relieved from any pain afterward, so there was nothing to worry about in that respect. They only mentioned possible discomfort and a sore throat from having the tubes during the operation.

They also advised that I would be confused after the anaesthetic—so even though they'd come and tell me how it went, and whether they were able to successfully complete the reconstruction, I likely wouldn't remember it. We laughed about it, and they said, "Let's see what you remember when you wake up." So I set myself up with a challenge—to try and remember what they told me when I woke up, just to prove them wrong. I had nothing better to do anyway!

It also helped knowing I was the first operation of the day. That meant I didn't have to wait too long, thinking and overthinking.

Due to an ongoing strike involving hospital support staff, there was uncertainty about whether my operation would proceed. The surgeons were ready, but they explained that nothing was guaranteed until I was in the theatre. It was likely the surgery could be pushed to Tuesday, after the bank holiday.

Around 9:00 AM, my surgeons arrived and said it was going ahead. I quickly messaged my family and handed over my personal belongings. It felt surreal—after everything, the moment had arrived.

I was wheeled through endless corridors and lifts, feeling disoriented in the maze-like hospital. Eventually, we reached the theatre. I met familiar staff and was asked to confirm the procedure: "Mastectomy of the right breast with immediate tummy flap reconstruction." I joked, "That's my right side, not yours," which made everyone laugh and helped lighten the mood.

Once I lay down, I silently asked my spiritual guides and

angels to be with me. Then the anaesthetic took over, and I drifted off.

That evening at 22:15, the hospital called my brother and my friend Klara to say I was stable and still under anaesthesia, about to move to recovery. The surgery had lasted 13 hours—longer than expected due to external delays, not surgical complications. The original estimate had been 9 hours, but that morning they had revised it to 10–12.

As I came to, I began registering sounds, lights, and voices. I was groggy, drifting in and out, but aware that I had made it to the other side. I saw a blurry lit picture on the wall, which looked like the sea. The nurses were checking vitals, typing, and chatting around me.

Suddenly, my plastic surgeon appeared and told me the operation had gone well. My first question was whether the breast had been reconstructed. He said yes. That was my biggest fear—that the reconstruction might fail and I would wake up without a breast. I felt deeply relieved.

Then my breast surgeon appeared, touched my shoulder, and offered reassurance. I focused hard on remembering those two conversations. Gradually, things became clearer, and I confirmed with a nurse that the sea picture I was seeing was real. They laughed and said they wished all their patients were as cheerful as I was.

Soon after, I was moved out of recovery. I said goodbye to the team, and they wheeled me through the hospital maze to my room.

Because of the nature of the operation—especially the need to keep my body temperature elevated to ensure the new blood vessels worked—I had a private room. It was essential for my recovery, and I felt grateful for the space and care.

26th August

I arrived in my hospital room just before midnight. The nurse asked if I wanted her to call anyone, and I realised my family might still be waiting for news. She called my friend Klara and my brother but only reached Klara. My mum doesn't speak English, but the nurse kindly held my phone so I could speak with her. She reassured me that everyone had already been informed—all was well.

After my 13-hour "beauty sleep" in theatre, I felt alert and started journaling. I had no pain and was given a control button for IV (Intravenous) pain relief. I couldn't eat yet but was given cold water with a straw. Nurses checked on me—and the flap—every hour, listening for blood flow in the reconstructed breast to ensure it was alive.

Because of the frequent checks, the night passed quickly. I stayed in a positive mental space, just as I had programmed myself to be. I admired the wall pictures and told myself I was content, even if not exactly happy. I avoided looking at the operated area—I was scared of how it might look and didn't want to feel heartbroken.

I didn't sleep much, likely because of the earlier anaesthesia and being in a new environment. Asking for help felt foreign; I'm used to managing everything myself. My ears were still blocked, making it hard to hear the nurses, though lying down helped slightly. My throat was sore, as expected.

The room was heated to 43°C, with an inflatable duvet constantly pumping hot air to keep me warm for flap viability. I imagined I was on a tropical holiday to cope.

By morning, I was able to message my mum and later called my dad. One of my plastic surgeons visited early, followed by the lead surgeon later. It was comforting to see them. They encouraged me to do hourly breathing exercises to expand my lungs and gave advice on safe arm movement, which I had been cautious about.

They reminded me that the next few days were critical—the transferred blood vessels needed to stay alive for the reconstruction to be successful. Constant monitoring and high warmth were key.

I told my surgeon I remembered asking whether the reconstruction had worked. Laughing, he said, "You actually asked if we moved your tummy fat into your breast!"—not quite how I remembered it.

Though I was very tired, I could communicate and chose not to make many calls because my voice was fading. My friend Klara visited and brought fresh juice—exactly what I needed. I could drink only juice, tea, coffee, or water, but being wrapped in warmth made hot drinks unappealing. I avoided sugary hospital juices, so Klara's freshly squeezed apple juice was perfect.

As Klara was leaving the ward, she asked which way to exit. I confidently told her they brought me in through the door behind me. She laughed—there was no door there, just a wall. I could've sworn I remembered double doors opening. It was a strange moment, realising how the mind can distort reality after anaesthesia.

Though I'd been told someone would help me stand, no one came. I was getting very hungry but had to wait 24 hours post-op for solid food, in case I needed to return to theatre. Finally, at 10 PM, I had a delicious vegan dinner. The nurse brought me a second sandwich for later.

I slept deeply and only woke at 4 AM to eat the saved sandwich, then fell back asleep.

27th August

Klara picked up my mum from the airport and brought fresh juice for me in the morning—just what I needed. Since I hadn't pre-ordered meals, lunch was improvised with Brussels sprouts, swede, and potatoes. Not exciting, but appreciated after fasting from Thursday evening until Saturday night.

Later, a nurse helped me stand and sit in a chair. But after sitting for a few minutes, I fainted—likely due to low blood pressure after 53 hours in bed. Afterward, a physio helped me walk a few steps and start breathing and arm exercises. The most painful part was a sore drain site. I was also given medication to lower the pain, taking care to avoid allergens.

The rest of the afternoon was uncomfortable. I had frequent bowel movements and couldn't go alone, needing to call nurses each time. This felt very unpleasant and degrading.

My mum arrived later, stayed until 8 PM, and helped where she could. I had several accidents and needed to be changed. The nurses suspected the reaction was from the brown tablet or possibly the antibiotics.

28th August

The hospital was quieter due to the bank holiday. The brown tablets were discontinued, but my bowel issues worsened, with painful cramps and continued diarrhoea. I described the pain as "giving birth to triangle-shaped hedgehogs." A nurse washed me, which helped me feel a bit better, but I still felt helpless and frustrated. Though I was promised a doctor, no one came.

My mum visited again—travelling alone on the UK train

system for the first time—and brought fresh juice. I continued needing help with the toilet, which was hard emotionally. I skipped dinner and asked for it to be saved.

Later that evening, a nurse came to disconnect my intravenous pain relief. I panicked, thinking I still needed it, but she told me I hadn't used it in two days—I had only pressed the button once. That surprised and encouraged me. I had managed the pain without realising it. Despite all the frustration, that discovery made me feel stronger and gave me a boost.

Later, around 9 PM, I was finally up for some food and ate my dinner. Luckily, after that, I fell asleep and slept until the next morning.

29th August

It was Tuesday, the first working day since I'd been on the ward. I had slept well and was feeling better.

The doctors came to see me. They had originally planned to take my drains out, but because of the diarrhoea, they said the readings could be misleading, so they decided to wait until the next day. They took the inflatable heated blanket off me and just kept me in a warm room, as the reconstruction and flap looked very good. The doctors—including my breast surgeon, who also came to see me that morning—were very happy with everything.

The nurses washed me, then helped me stand up and spend a couple of hours sitting in a chair instead of lying in bed. I undid the curtains and watched the world outside.

I was able to walk to the toilet now, but I still had the catheter, so I needed someone to help carry everything. But if

I had another bowel movement, I could now use the toilet—which was better. Luckily, I only needed to go a few times, usually after meals, so things were settling.

My friend Sandra was going to come see me, but someone she had been around had a suspected case of COVID, so we decided it was better to just catch up over the phone. Later, my friends Ed and Sarah came to see me in the afternoon, so the day went by quickly. Suddenly, a lot was happening.

That night, I left the curtains open and could see a large car park lit up in neon rainbow colours. It might sound crazy, but it felt very calming—like looking at a Christmas tree. The view from the hospital wasn't nice—there was no view of the city of Cambridge or of nature. But this gave it a completely different vibe.

And really, the way we experience life is how we choose to make it. I wanted to experience peace, calmness, and positivity. And even if there wasn't anything fancy around—even a lit-up car park would do. We need to find the little things.

Enjoy the little things in life, for one day you'll look back and realise they were the big things

ROBERT BRAULT

30th August – A Big Step Forward

The day started with a big step: having the catheter taken out so I could finally start going to the toilet on my own.

A specialist nurse from Plastic Surgery came to check on me and apply new dressings. I asked her to make sure I wouldn't see anything, as I was still scared to look. She gently spoke to me and suggested that I might be expecting it to look much worse than it actually was.

My friend Lisa came to visit me in the morning. She had recently been to San Francisco, Yosemite, Death Valley, the Grand Canyon, and Las Vegas. She had so many photos, and I love travelling and seeing new places—so I really enjoyed her showing me all the beautiful places she'd visited on her holiday.

In the afternoon, a nurse came to remove two of the drains. They gave me morphine first to ease any pain the drains might cause during removal. It was a very strange sensation—I could feel it moving through one side of my body to the other.

I also brushed my teeth for the first time since being in hospital, and that helped me start to feel a little more like myself again.

My mum came to visit in the afternoon. While she was there, the specialist nurse from Plastic Surgery returned and took me out of the room for a walk. She walked me through the corridor—it was the first time I'd left the room. When we came back, I noticed just how warm the room actually was.

I had thought about watching TV or a film that evening, but I couldn't believe it cost £10 for one day or £24 for three days to use the hospital's TV service. I found out it was only free in the morning. I could have paid it, but it didn't feel right that patients had to pay that much for entertainment. So instead, I watched something on Amazon Prime on my phone.

With two of the drains gone (one from the side/back and the other from the right side of my tummy), I realised I had originally thought the only painful area was where they took the lymph nodes out—but it turned out one of the drains was causing that pain. Once they removed the drain on my side, it felt much better.

But then I started to feel pain on the left side of my tummy, or just below it, and I had to ask for painkillers. Due to my allergies, they gave me 10 ml of morphine. It tasted like some sweets from my childhood, and I slept like a baby.

31st August

The specialist nurse and my plastic surgeon came to see me in the morning and confirmed that the reconstruction had been a success. They said they would request the remaining drains be removed, and that I might be able to go home in the afternoon—but they hadn't confirmed it yet.

So, one of my manifestations was done: the reconstruction worked!

The second manifestation I had been visualising was for the lymph nodes they removed during the mastectomy to come back as non-cancerous. The results from the lab were expected in about two weeks, so there was still a wait.

They gave me some morphine and removed the remaining drains. This felt even worse than the previous ones—I could literally feel the sensation moving through my whole body. It was something I'd never experienced before—probably the strangest physical feeling I've ever had.

Afterwards, a rehabilitation nurse came to guide me through some physiotherapy exercises and was going to teach me how to manage stairs. But as we set off for our walk, I fainted, so we didn't get there. It had been right after the drains were taken out, and that's what caused me to pass out.

Later, another nurse came to wash me, and by then it was lunchtime.

Since I'm allergic to most painkillers, they had to look for an alternative. They couldn't send me home with morphine, so they decided to try codeine or something similar. Because of my past allergic reactions, they decided it would be safer for me to stay one more night in hospital—just in case I had a reaction to the new medication.

Now I knew I was going home the next morning.

I was quite tired after lunch. So much had gone on that day—after they took the drains out and I fainted in the hallway—so I just lay in bed, meditating and even drifting away. I had some ideas about how I could help other women going through a similar journey in the future.

The specialist nurse from plastic surgery came to help me put on the post-operative bra and pants. My mum and my friend arrived around 4:00 PM and spent a couple of hours with me before my other friends, Becky and Stuart, came to visit.

Later, I watched a film on my phone, then took the codeine and slept well until the morning.

Second week of recovery – from 1st September

I woke up remembering a dream about my cousin. We wanted to go to the cemetery to visit our grandma's grave, and we saw a beautiful rainbow light there—as a sign from her. There's a big thing that runs in my family—mainly between me and my mum. Something significant always seems to happen in our lives when we dream about grandma. But I couldn't make sense of it this time. I thought maybe it was about being discharged from the hospital, so I just left it there.

A nurse came to wash me before breakfast. The doctors came to see me and confirmed they were happy for me to go home. The specialist nurse and physio arrived around the same time. The physio asked a lot of questions about the operation, which led to an interesting conversation. I learned that a nipple-sparing mastectomy is only done if, from an oncological point of view, there are no concerns—such as cancer being close to the nipple—or if it's a preventative mastectomy with a reconstruction.

But they are able to reconstruct a nipple by cutting skin from the upper inner thigh, where the texture is similar to that of a nipple and areola. They cut two shapes—a circle for the areola and another shape that reminded me of a winner's podium. That shape is rolled and formed into a nipple. I found it so interesting.

They also gave me a seatbelt protector to place over my chest for car journeys—both when being driven and later when I'd start driving myself.

I was told I would be discharged around 11 AM. My mum arrived at the hospital between 10 and 11 to help me with everything. I was finally discharged just before lunchtime. I said thank you and goodbye to everyone on the ward. They were all amazing and took such good care of me. There were one or two days where I had a nurse whose attitude I didn't quite like—she seemed a bit confused—but it was nothing major.

What was very interesting was that many nurses and doctors kept telling me that I didn't look like someone who had just had major surgery—I was in such good spirits the whole time. But that was because I chose to be. I accepted that I was going to be in hospital, but I wanted to feel good about it.

The first night, I remember thinking that the room didn't even feel like a hospital room. And then one of my friends, when they came to visit, said, "Wow, you can really tell from the design and everything that this is a hospital." Same place, two different people, two different experiences. I hadn't seen it that way at the time. I had created my own reality—focusing on the nice pictures that lifted me up and the lit-up car park outside. Everything is about how you choose to experience it.

We took the lift downstairs and waited at the reception for our taxi. When it arrived, it was a very comfortable, quite luxurious car. But even so, I could feel every little bump and hump in my tummy.

We got home around 1 PM and had some lunch.

In the early days of recovery, I felt physically okay—so the hardest part was holding back. As someone always on the move, it was challenging not to do everyday tasks like lifting a bag or cooking. I wasn't allowed to lift anything heavier than a kettle with two cups of water, and had to constantly pause to think before doing anything. My mum helped with tasks I'd normally do in seconds, which tested my patience.

It was a hot week—around 30°C—and I had to wear multiple layers: supportive post-op pants with hooks and zippers, a compression garment over that, a surgical bra, and knee-high compression socks. The socks caused evening leg twitches, so my mum would take them off at bedtime and slip them back on while I was half-asleep.

Despite the warm weather, I couldn't enjoy being outside much. My movement was limited, and every step strained my tummy. Walking within the house was manageable, but going outside was out of the question. I was advised to do no more than light movement during the second week post-op (first week at home). I averaged 2,000–3,000 steps per day and only did hospital-prescribed physio exercises.

Showering wasn't possible yet due to taped scars on my breast and tummy. I napped in the afternoons, always on my back, using a triangle pillow for elevation and support.

One of the hardest parts emotionally was not being able to sleep with my cat, Max. I had to shut myself in the spare room for safety, and he would scratch at the door, not understanding why he couldn't be near me. I missed him terribly.

Nutrition became a focus again. I resumed juicing—especially pineapple juice, rich in bromelain to aid healing. I finished my antibiotics and started probiotics and oat milk kefir to restore gut health, still recovering from chemotherapy. I also added detox-supporting supplements like Amla and medicinal mushrooms. My blocked ear even began to improve that week.

At the start of the new month, I did my usual monthly reflection. August had been beautiful despite everything: my trip to Malta, time with family, swimming with a dolphin—a childhood dream fulfilled. My hair and eyebrows had started to regrow. I found peace again, a deep sense of love and self-acceptance.

I felt proud of myself. The little scared girl inside had faced surgery calmly and came through it in good spirits—even the doctors were surprised at how well I handled it. I continued journaling in hospital, confident that I would one day write a book. I even came up with its title.

And finally—my tummy was flat. For the first time ever. I had written in January that one of my goals was to get a flat tummy. I imagined it would come from exercise or diet, not breast reconstruction. Still, I was grateful for the fat I had once disliked—because it gave me a natural-looking new breast.

Knowing I could do very little physically, I chose not to be frustrated by it but to work mentally instead. I spent time visualising myself being cancer-free and recovering surprisingly well from the operation.

I chose to fill the first two weeks by repeating the Silva Method Basic Course. It was running across two weeks—four afternoons between 1 and 5 PM. When you're a Silva Method graduate, you can repeat the entire course for a fraction of the price. So I did it. I entertained myself in the second and third weeks of recovery with something that helped me to anchor what I had learned several months ago and to enhance my manifestation abilities.

I also decided to book in to repeat the Life Purpose Advanced Course on 27th September, which I had done back in January just before I got diagnosed. I had gained an insight into what my purpose might be, and I wanted to see what answers I would get this time, now that I was more clearly set on my path.

Another big step I took was deciding to start studying for the British citizenship test. I had been in the UK for 10 years, and it was just about time.

On top of all that, my legal cover insurance claim was accepted, and I started to collaborate with my new solicitors regarding the Employment Tribunal.

So I was suddenly busy and had some goals and things to work on while recovering.

I finished the second week of recovery, on 7th September, with my first check-up at the hospital in the Plastic Surgery unit. They cut some stitches that were sticking out—the rest were dissolvable. They changed the tape and applied less tape than before. And the nurse was right when she said I probably imagined it to look much worse than it actually did. It looked pretty good—and it still looked like a breast, like a beautiful breast with some plasters on it.

Never be ashamed of a scar. It simply means you were stronger than whatever tried to hurt you.

UNKNOWN

I had to wear the compression socks for another week, unfortunately, but I was allowed to have a quick shower—making sure not to wet my breast too much yet. I reached a post-operation record on Thursday and did 4,700 steps around my home and the hospital.

Third week of recovery - from 8th September

I was adding more steps in very slowly and did a bigger loop on Saturday, 9th September. It measured 0.5 kilometres, but I still only did 2,600 steps.

I continued doing the Silva Method course during this week, and we started to take little walks, only in the street where I live—five minutes of very slow walking. So, taking baby steps. Towards the end of week 3 of recovery, I had my first small victory—leaving our street and walking to a nearby shop and back. Still at snail's pace, but I did it!

I focused on checking all the criteria for citizenship, and I was helping my mum with cooking (just very lightly), helping her put things together the way I wanted them—as my dietary requirements were completely different from hers. She could do with a little guidance (and me being a little annoying by telling her exactly how I wanted things!).

I also talked to my manager about a potential collaboration after my prolonged notice period ends. This was very positive, as I wanted to try something different. I was thinking about continuing in my line of work but on a contractual basis rather than as an employee. My idea was that it could enable me to earn more, operate as a business, and work half the year—spending the rest of the time developing the property business, publishing a book, and helping other women affected by breast cancer. I wasn't sure how it would all manifest.

Fourth week of recovery - from 15th September

The first thing I did as soon as week 4 started was to take off the compression knee socks. What a relief!

This week I deep-dived into studying for the citizenship exam, and Klara and I really started to work on the property business—beginning to look for properties we could rent from landlords and operate as short-term lets, charging by nightly rate and generating cashflow that way. We also started to explore how we could purchase our own property using a combination of commercial financing and private investor funds. We had been laying the foundation for a few months—on and off, given my situation and treatments—but now it was becoming real.

Unfortunately, my hearing got worse again, and I was really pressing the support nurses to book me in to be looked at. My ears were still blocked after the weekend, so apart from some short-term improvement, they had been like that since the last chemotherapy. I tried using ear drops to clear it, but nothing changed. They finally expedited the process and booked me straight in for Tuesday, 19th September—only a few days away. It was very annoying.

I also asked about the lab results I had been impatiently waiting for—to see what they found in my tissue and lymph nodes and what this would mean for further treatments and aftercare. I still visualised every day, several times a day, that I was cancer-free, in remission, and discharged from medical care.

No results were back yet, though. Apparently, there was a delay, but they should be available by my appointment at the breast clinic on 25th September.

My friend Sandra came to see me at the weekend and took me out for lunch. It was still fairly warm in the middle of September, and we sat outside to eat. Later, my brother, sister-in-law, and nephew came to visit—plus the unborn baby too!

I also had a call with my close friends in the Czech Republic. So, it was a weekend full of socialising.

Finally, I had the appointment at audiology, but they did a lot of hearing tests without giving me any answers. They said I needed to speak to a consultant and would receive an invitation for that.

We stopped in Ely on the way home for a nice, warming lunch. We had to use taxis that day but luckily got a generous discount from someone I knew.

The next day, we changed the tapes on my scars, and everything looked much nicer and tidier. I was also preparing my outfit for my friend's wedding.

I finished the week 4 with attending my friend Becky's wedding, looking great and also being able to fit in the dress I bought back in summer. But it was a challenge to fit into it with all the supportive clothing and garment. My friend Sandra came to pick me up. We had an amazing time at the wedding and met a lot of other friends and colleagues there and it was all beautiful and quite emotional too. Sandra took me home too.

Fifth week of recovery - from 22nd September

I started this week by planting some tulips in front of my house—something I had wanted to do for a few years, but it was always too late to plant them in time for the next spring.

It was Monday morning, 25th September 2023, and it was a big day. I had two appointments: first at the Plastic Surgery unit early in the morning, then I was meeting Sandra at the hospital. She accompanied me and my mum to the Breast Clinic for the results and to find out what the next steps would be.

I couldn't get any reasonable lift, so we decided to combine a lift with trains. My friend Klara took us to the train station in the village, and we took a train to Cambridge, where we got a taxi to the hospital.

The check-up at Plastic Surgery went really well. The only disappointment was when I mentioned that I had marked in my calendar the day I could drive again—counting six weeks from the operation. They advised that it might be more like eight weeks rather than six and recommended trying just driving in my street first to see how I feel, and then starting to drive very small distances, maybe just around the village, before getting fully back to it. I had been so excited about getting back to driving, and this was something I didn't expect—but in the grand scheme of things, it wasn't that bad.

The booklet said that for this type of operation it was six weeks without driving. I love driving and need to be in movement for my thoughts to flow and my emotions to process. As an independent woman, driving is an essential part of my freedom. I even marked the day of completion of the first six weeks after the operation in my calendar with a car sticker.

About four weeks post-op, I saw my plastic surgeon. Though I felt fine, he strongly advised waiting closer to eight weeks before driving. He cited risks like emergency stops or sudden movements that could affect the reconstruction, as well as potential insurance issues if I were in an accident. I was advised to ease into driving after six weeks, starting with short practice sessions near home, ideally with someone accompanying me.

I was also cleared to stop using the surgical tapes and could begin moisturising my scars. I had a bottle of bio oil ready.

Before my next Breast Clinic appointment, Sandra met us at the car park. I was anxious but focused on visualising clear lymph nodes and accepting that all the cancer had been removed. My mum stayed in the waiting room since she doesn't speak English, and I wanted to focus fully during the consultation.

Inside, the surgeon greeted me and reviewed the operation and lab results. He said I had a pathological complete response—meaning no active cancer cells were found in any of the tissue or lymph nodes removed. I was stunned. On the day of the operation, I had already been cancer-free.

This was exactly what I had visualised and programmed for since diagnosis. I thought I had failed when the 31 July scan still showed 3mm, but I had actually manifested the result—I just wasn't meant to know it until now. I wept with joy. It was the happiest moment of my life and my greatest achievement.

Afterwards, we discussed the next steps. There was the option of radiotherapy to the lymph nodes, though it came with an increased risk of lymphedema. Radiotherapy to the breast or chest wall was recommended. I would also continue with fourteen more Phesgo injections, having already completed four during chemotherapy. Finally, there was the plan for ten years of hormone therapy pills

I knew I didn't want the lymph node radiotherapy. I felt okay about chest radiotherapy and Phesgo, though I wanted to speak to an oncologist for more details. I was uneasy about the hormone pills, feeling they contradicted my healing lifestyle. But I reminded myself: if I had manifested complete remission, I could find a path through this too.

The surgeon examined my reconstructed breast and was very pleased with the results. As I got dressed, I asked when I'd see him next. He smiled and said, "I hope never." We laughed.

Sandra and I returned to the waiting room, crying with joy. My mum saw us and also cried—uncertain at first—until we told her the news: I was cancer-free, even before the operation.

We all hugged and cried our way back to the car. Sandra dropped us at my favourite vegan restaurant, and Mum and I had a celebratory lunch. I didn't want alcohol, but she had an espresso martini. I tasted a drop—just for fun—and found it awful. Chemo had changed my taste and sensitivity completely.

I still couldn't believe it. I kept wondering what the moment of healing had been. I thought back to Malta—when the dolphin splashed me. That deep feeling of unconditional love and spiritual connection may have been it.

I was officially declared in remission on 25 September, but I had achieved it spiritually and physically between 31 July and 25 August—without even knowing.

We took a taxi home, and because it was a nice dry sunny day, we decided to take a little walk. We walked just around the block and suddenly saw a rainbow light in the middle of a blue sky—just above my house. It was like a sign from the Universe, a message that the angels and my spiritual guides had been with me. That this is where one journey ends, and another begins.

It also reminded me of the rainbow I saw in my dream on the last day in the hospital—that was connected to my grandma. It felt like she is looking after me from the other side. And that she's been doing that my whole life.

When it rains, look for rainbows.
When it's dark, look for stars

OSCAR WILDE

The next day, I was doing some research and found that the tablets they wanted to prescribe for the next 10 years might have many side effects—one of them being an increased risk of uterine cancer. So, I didn't feel comfortable with it. I started to put together a list of questions regarding the next steps and after-treatments in preparation for my upcoming appointment at the oncology department on 12th October.

I also started to expand on my walks slightly.

On the 27th and 28th of September, I repeated the Life Mission course, and it was interesting to compare the notes from the previous course I took just before the diagnosis.

Here is what came up for me in January and in September 2023—before and after cancer:

January 2023 (before cancer)	September 2023 (after cancer)
What is my life purpose?	
Lead, teach a lot of people, partnerships, share, help, guide, believe	Lead, inspire but don't tell people what to do – inspire them to change their habits; care about others where you are needed, care about yourself. Creating business not for income only but for a contribution to the society

January 2023 (before cancer)	**September 2023 (after cancer)**
Who do I need to become?	
Confident speaker, open to people and relationships, overcome fear of judgement, accept myself, trust myself, stop worrying about outcomes, enjoy what I am doing	You have everything now. Start. Slow down. Stop going through a task list. Prioritise your purpose first.
What do I need to release?	
Fear, fear of being hurt, fear of being unlucky, expectation of bad scenarios, focusing on what if, fear of not being enough, being judged, fear of being stupid, being wrong, fear of not being loved and accepted	Fear. Endless task list. Rush.
What must I embrace?	
Joy, deep relationships with people, quality relationships, listening skills, empathy, How can I help?, Trust that if something does or doesn't happen I am just being redirected	Interact with people. Self-confidence. Trust. Listen. Connect.
Is there anything else I need to know?	
No. The right information comes when you will need it.	All is well. You have a huge support. Everyone is believing in you. Do not compare yourself to others. THE BOOK is the answer! Listen to alpha and theta sounds whilst writing.

This is actually phenomenal. As these were things I was working on throughout the cancer journey without even realising it and without an intention. The right information came to me when I needed it and it was a couple of days away. Something did happen – diagnosis, the job offer withdrawal – it was the redirection! I didn't read the previous sheet before doing this exercise in September but when I compare it, it all makes sense. And when I am writing it now and sharing this it all makes even more sense. It makes sense why things happened certain way. I am absolutely guided every step of the way!

Sixth week of recovery - from 29th September

We started this week of recovery by taking a taxi to Ely. We did some shopping and also went to a sushi restaurant. I couldn't eat sushi during chemotherapy because it contains raw fish, and I had been looking forward to having some after a long time. We had a great time, and it marked the end of my mum's visit for the year—otherwise, we could get into trouble with immigration.

The next day, Klara took my mum to the airport, and then she and I stopped for a nice meal in Cambridge.

When I got back home, it suddenly hit me—a feeling of realisation that I love my house and my garden, but it's a bit sad not having anyone to share it with. After my mum left, I really felt how nice it is to have someone to share life with. That was when I decided to make a change in my approach and how I felt about dating sites, and I started to look for someone to date online.

It was against my beliefs—I've always thought that when you're meant to meet someone, you'll bump into them, even in the most ridiculous place. And that did happen to me a few times. In fact, the most ridiculous place I ever met someone was when I met my amazing friend Klara, who is now also my business partner—we met at the post office! So I knew I wasn't wrong to believe in serendipity, but I still felt like I wanted to increase my chances of meeting someone.

It might sound a bit crazy—I had just been through breast

cancer, one of the cancers that affects intimate relationships and confidence the most when it comes to starting a new relationship. But you know what? I didn't care. I knew I was, and still am, the hero of my own story.

I decided to be completely open about it when I decide to meet someone in person, because I wanted them to also feel that they had the choice to walk away without me taking it personally. I wanted someone who would be okay with it. And if they weren't, I'd be okay with that too—because that would mean they weren't the right person for me, and I wasn't the right person for them.

Interestingly, I also knew I didn't have to lower my expectations just because I had a mastectomy. I had a reconstruction, but it was still going to take some time before they would be able to reconstruct my nipple as well. These are big things—but only as big as the meaning I give to them. People lose confidence over smaller things than this. So why should I stop myself from dating just because of what I had been through?

I also started phasing back into work slowly.

As usual, I was reviewing the last month and doing some reflection. I was pleased that I chose personal development and growth during my recovery time. I finally had the time and mental capacity to start learning for the citizenship test, which I had been thinking about for a while.

But the biggest win of all was finding out I was cancer-free—and that I had manifested it before the operation without even knowing it.

Seventh week of recovery - from 6th October

I was at the beginning of my new journey and decided to do some things at home that I hadn't got around to doing before—either due to lack of time or money. So, I had a new fence put in, a new fitted door installed for my wardrobe in the bedroom, and my friend Ed and his partner came round and helped me hang a new bathroom cabinet that had been sitting under my sofa for many months. We finished by lunchtime and celebrated in a restaurant by the river, sitting outside! It was such a nice and warm autumn.

I started driving short distances in the village from Sunday, 8th October. Something I didn't expect was that every time I pressed the clutch to change gear, I could feel it inside my tummy. An automatic car would have definitely been helpful in this situation.

I had some great news on 10th October—my niece was born! What a date—10th of the 10th month!

On Thursday, 12th October, heading towards week 7 of my recovery, I had planned to drive just within the village to the train station, then take the train to Cambridge and use a taxi or bus to get to the hospital. When I got to the station, I found out that the service was disrupted. I could either take a taxi or drive myself. Since I was already feeling confident with short-distance driving, I decided to drive all the way. I got to the hospital in Cambridge, parked, and felt okay.

I thought the appointment was to discuss all my after-treatments. I had prepared a long list of about 20 questions so I could understand which after-treatments I'd feel comfortable with—but it turned out to be only with the radiology specialist. So, I didn't get all the answers I was hoping for. Again, I felt frustrated that no one was looking at me and my situation holistically. Each specialist only focused on their area. I was told that this wasn't "pick and choose"—that this is the whole after-treatment package.

I was surprised to be meeting only the radiologist that day. He talked me through the radiotherapy options. I explained that I didn't want radiotherapy on the lymph nodes but would consider radiotherapy for the chest wall (breast). That course would be 3 weeks—5 days a week. However, I wanted to speak to the oncologist because I needed to understand all the available options in order to make an informed decision. The radiologist was very understanding and told me I could take time to think about it and let them know when I was ready. He was the first medical professional who didn't object to the holistic methods I'd been using and was actually very supportive.

I drove back home, but that was when I started to feel pain in my tummy. I knew I had overstretched myself and shouldn't have driven that far.

Eighth week of recovery - from 13th October

Klara and I decided to start looking for a property to invest in, and we spent both Saturday and Sunday viewing properties in Norwich. It was a busy weekend—but exciting!

I had a call with my homeopath and complained about my blocked ears, which had been bothering me for over two months. She gave me some homeopathic remedies to clear them out. Within a few days, my ears cleared and I could hear better. Nothing else had helped—only the homeopathic remedy. Meanwhile, I still hadn't heard anything from audiology.

I also had my first professional cleaning done by a cleaner. I had arranged for cleaning support during my recovery to help with basic housework and changing the cat litter. It was a massive help.

I tried driving to Ely and back and started to drive more regularly. It seemed fine now. So, the plastic surgeon was right—it really did take 8 weeks to recover enough for that type of operation. It might have been doable earlier if I'd had an automatic car, as the greatest pressure was from pressing the clutch.

Nineth week of recovery - from 20th October

With regards to my physical body—my breast started to feel more like a breast again: softer, and more similar in texture to the other one. It was also beginning to look closer in size, although still slightly bigger. The hair under my armpit started regrowing. I could hear completely again, which felt amazing. I was finally able to return to my own bed and no longer had to keep the door closed to stop my cat from jumping on my operated areas.

I had another check-up at the plastic surgery clinic, and all was well. My next appointment wasn't scheduled until the new year.

I did quite a lot of driving this week, and everything went smoothly.

I had my first date through the online app. It went well—he was a very nice person and seemed completely fine with my situation, but I just didn't feel he was the right person for me. So, the journey continued.

I went on another date later the same week. We had a really nice chat, so I decided to see him again.

Tenth week of recovery - from 27th October

I started the week by visiting my homeopath and combining it with an in-person energy healing session—to energetically wash everything away and realign again.

I received a call from the oncologist to discuss my questions and concerns.

However, I found—yet again—that there is no holistic approach in conventional medicine. Radiotherapy and other treatments are completely disconnected, and you don't have a single person looking at your case as a whole.

But I had been using visualisations and Silva techniques to ask for guidance and answers—what the right after-treatments are, if any, for me.

And in this call, I was told that someone had made a mistake in my record, and that I don't need to take the hormonal therapy tablets for 10 years. That was one ruled out! A great answer from the Universe.

So I agreed to the HER2-targeted injection therapy, which will be every 3 weeks for another year, to help prevent the cancer from coming back. The numbers from the trials were significant, with a 40% higher chance of the cancer not returning. I had been concerned about the reaction seen on one of the CT scans back in April, when I was considered a suspect for pulmonary hypertension. So we agreed with the oncologist that they would do an ECG before starting the treatment, and during it, just to monitor my heart.

I also requested a further call from the radiology consultant, because I wasn't able to fit the 3 weeks of radiotherapy in as I originally thought—I had assumed this would already be done and dusted by now. I had booked a trip to Edinburgh at the end of November, an Angelic Reiki course at the beginning of December, and then visits to my family in the Czech Republic and Slovakia. The oncologist told me that radiotherapy should happen within 3 months of the operation. So the delay was caused by me not just following what I was told. I very much need to be in control of things—especially because it's my body, and I know that western medicine doesn't take everything into account. It's far from holistic.

So then I waited for a call from the radiology team regarding the scheduling challenge. I told myself that if they could accommodate my holiday, then I would do it. If not, then I wouldn't—and I'd take that as a sign from the Universe. And they did accommodate me. They said I could start after the 15th of December and do the 3-week course over Christmas, going to the hospital for 10 minutes every weekday.

So although I set that up to help me with my decision, I still wasn't sure—there was still something at the back of my mind questioning it. Looking back, I can see I used the holiday as an excuse. I was delaying the decision. It was the same situation I had before the operation. It's like I was unable to make the decision myself. I knew I didn't want to do any harm to my body with radiation, and I also didn't want to be in a situation where I opted out and then the cancer came back. And the truth is, I would never know whether I made the right decision or not.

It also felt daunting to go to the hospital every day—that didn't create positive feelings, especially over Christmas. But I was going to do it. Still, something kept haunting me about it.

My reflection on the month was that it marked a new and amazing start—with viewing properties and truly feeling like we can do this and build a property business. I also wrote the first section of this book. And mainly, I was healing well. I felt so blessed and fortunate again.

Eleventh week of recovery - from 3rd November

We went for another full day of property viewings in Norwich and came across a little wig shop nearby. Although my hair had already started to regrow, I went for a complete change and bought a dark brown wig—a bob with a fringe. We were laughing because I showed up to our viewings with different hair just to confuse the estate agents!

I also went on another date, but again, I didn't feel it was going anywhere—we just weren't the right fit.

This week I had my citizenship test, and I passed with almost all the answers correct—maybe one wrong. That was a relief. I still had to do the English exam, which is a very basic test that I could not possibly fail after living and working in the UK for 10 years, but it was part of the process.

Twelfth week of recovery - from 10th November

I had my ECG done prior to starting the Phesgo injections, and apparently, it showed that my heart was perfect—like something straight out of a textbook, ideal for demonstrating to students.

I spent the entire weekend with my friend Klara watching a 2-day online course on how to invest in property, and we signed up for a 12-month program to get us started.

With all this great news, I decided to finish this section here—on 16th November, which marked the officially stated recovery time for this type of operation. But there was never truly a specific date for recovery. It all phased out gradually, and I was slowly returning to "normal"—well, that's not true. That's how I imagined it at first. But there was never a going back to normal.

There was only a transition to a new normal—a normal that has never felt "normal" in any way.

VIII

Radiotherapy, Aftertreatments & The New "Normal"

16th November

I had agreed over the phone with the doctor to proceed with radiotherapy of the breast, but not the lymph nodes. I went in for a pre-radiotherapy CT scan, knowing in the back of my mind that I still wasn't fully decided. I was waiting for a sign from the Universe.

When I arrived at the CT scan room, they asked me to sign the consent form. I explained I wasn't ready because I had some concerns. The radiologist asked what they were, but when he said they didn't want to proceed with the scan unless I was sure, I broke down in tears. I hadn't expected to be pressured into making a final decision on the spot.

They called in a consultant, who listened patiently as I shared my concerns—not just about side effects, but about the emotional toll of returning to hospital again for three weeks. I had visualised the hospital leaving my life. Chemo and surgery had been intense but focused. This felt different—like the easiest part of the treatment plan had become the hardest. It felt like going backward. I doubted my mental resilience to handle the cumulative effects of radiotherapy and the post-treatment fatigue.

The consultant consulted a colleague and came back with a clarification—they had assumed I had implants, which is why three weeks had been mentioned. But because my reconstruction used my own tissue, a one-week course would be sufficient. The radiation dose would be the same, only the schedule was shorter.

This explained a lot, including the earlier confusion about potentially needing another surgery. If I hadn't stayed actively involved in my care, I might have ended up with unnecessary treatments—including hormone pills for 10 years or the wrong length of radiotherapy.

I agreed to the one-week course, which we scheduled to begin after my trips to Edinburgh and Czechia/Slovakia, still within the three-month post-op window. The consultant also recommended a gel to protect my skin and explained that side effects might increase after treatment, not necessarily during.

She offered a hug, which I accepted. A student who had been present found me afterward and reassured me with kind words, reminding me that it was okay to question things and that I had done the right thing.

I signed the consent form and completed the CT planning scan. They tattooed three small reference dots—one in the middle and one on each side. It was a sharp scratch but painless. Afterward, I was emotional again when I received a small gift box with thoughtful, plant-based and natural items for breast cancer patients. It was a touching gesture.

I felt at peace with my decision and happy that the treatment would start on 18 December and finish before Christmas.

17th – 30th November

The rest of the month was uplifting. Klara and I started a property coaching membership and were excited to learn and connect with others. I also sorted out my English exam for UK citizenship.

We travelled to Edinburgh for a weekend and visited the Christmas market. It was a lovely trip—if not for the cold, I could imagine living there.

At the end of November, one of our property coaches announced a 100-day challenge to build good habits, including 30 minutes of exercise daily. I realised I had become too inactive post-surgery and decided to join. I started walking and doing light workouts in my living room every day. The challenge helped me get back into a rhythm with exercise.

1st – 17th December

The first weekend of December, I re-sat an Angelic Reiki course with Mel, which I had first done in 2020. I planned to take the Master course the following year and felt this would help me release what no longer served me and deepen my spiritual connection. After the second attunement, I felt a strong connection to my grandma, as if she had been looking after me all along. I saw a ray of rainbow light again, just like the day I was told I was cancer-free. I cried—not from sadness or joy, but from a deep spiritual connection, feeling God, the Universe, and the angels within me. I brought home a purple crystal from the course, and when I placed it on my shelf, a rainbow light appeared again. Now, every time I do Reiki healing, the rainbow ray appears above me.

My last working day was officially 15 December, but I used some leave and finished in the first week of December, before my trip to Czechia and Slovakia. I travelled on 7 December and spent time with friends and family. I accompanied my dad to receive a special award for his lifetime contribution to music, then met my mum in Prague and travelled together to Slovakia to visit more family. It was a beautiful trip, and I especially loved Prague at Christmas—it's magical.

I returned on 14 December and spent the next day viewing properties in Norwich. On Sunday the 17th, we celebrated Christmas at our favourite vegan restaurant in Cambridge and visited a National Trust light trail. I felt like I was living again after a difficult year and ready to finish radiotherapy the next week and start fresh, both personally and professionally.

That night, I got home around 9 PM. Max greeted me, happy to see me. I fed him and went upstairs. While I was upstairs, I suddenly heard a terrible scream. I ran down to find Max unable to walk—his leg was injured. One of the kitchen drawers hadn't closed properly, as sometimes happened, and it must have reopened. I believe Max jumped from the worktop, and his leg got caught in the drawer rails.

Usually, I closed the kitchen gate so he couldn't enter unsupervised, but this time I hadn't. I felt awful. I called an emergency vet and brought him in. They kept him overnight, and he was clearly in pain. I got home around midnight. The house felt empty without him. I prayed for him before I fell asleep.

18th December

I woke up and saw a rainbow outside my window. I had seen rainbows throughout my healing journey and took it as a sign that Max would be okay.

It was a difficult morning, but I tried to refocus. I went for lunch with Sandra, then prepared for my first radiotherapy session. I applied the gel prescribed to protect my skin.

During lunch, the vet called and said Max likely had a displaced knee and needed a specialist orthopaedist. They arranged for him to go to a specialist clinic on Wednesday and would send him home with pain relief in the meantime.

I scheduled everything so I could attend radiotherapy first, then pick up Max on the way home. That worked out. He was distressed and had bald spots on his paw—possibly from something spilled on him. The clinic had also overcharged me—over £1,000 for one night and an X-ray—but thankfully, I had pet insurance.

Back at home, Max was hobbling on three legs but seemed relieved. I was glad to have him home but wished he were already at the clinic getting the help he needed for his knee.

19th December

We were home on Tuesday, but I went to the hospital for my treatment and returned home afterwards.

20th December

I continued writing this book and scheduled one hour first thing in the morning every day to do that. I took Max to the specialist clinic later in the morning. It was a private clinic, and I knew he would be in good hands there. Still, I felt very emotional leaving him.

On the way home, I visited a National Trust site just to clear my head and to get my walking in for the day. Then I went to Cambridge to do some shopping and attend my radiotherapy.

21st December

It was Thursday, and they were going to operate on Max. I tried to fill in my citizenship application that I had started some time ago but found that I needed two references, and one person had to meet specific requirements and fill in paperwork — so it was another thing to sort out.

Max had undergone the operation and was recovering well, but they wanted to monitor him for a few more days before discharging him from the clinic. I was advised that I would need a dog cage and to keep him in it for several weeks to prevent him from jumping and causing any damage to his operated knee.

I posted on Facebook, and my friend Becky was so kind to lend me hers. I went to pick it up on the way home from my afternoon treatment.

22nd December

It was Friday, the day of my last radiotherapy session, and this time my treatment was first thing in the morning — which was great, as I could have it all done and dusted. I arranged to visit Max on the way back from Cambridge. The vets said they don't normally allow visits, but I insisted.

I then prepared everything at home for Max to return and started a program on Mindvalley called Lifebook, where I defined how I wanted my life to look in all areas. This became my focus over Christmas because I was at a crossroads in life and wanted to start crafting the life I truly wanted.

I had been so absorbed by everything going on with Max the whole week that I was completely distracted from focusing on any side effects or feelings during the radiotherapy treatment. The only thing I did was visualise both me and Max feeling well and healthy every morning and evening. I also visualised during radiotherapy that the rays were doing great things — eliminating the cancer while protecting my body from any side effects.

But it was exhausting enough to run to the hospital and back every day just for a week. Doing that for three weeks would have been much more challenging, especially as the side effects would likely start kicking in during that time.

23rd December

I finally went to pick up Max, and it was nice to have him home — even though I had several challenging weeks ahead, keeping him in the crate while I recovered from radiotherapy.

My treatment had finished, but now I started to feel a kind of tiredness I hadn't experienced before.

24th – 31st December

It was a quiet time — Christmas with my brother, sister-in-law, her mum, and their children. I saw a friend one day and used the time to reflect and craft a detailed vision for my future life in the form of the Lifebook. The tiredness gradually increased, but it wasn't so severe that I couldn't push through and do things. It didn't stop me, but I definitely rested more, took it easier, and was usually in bed very early.

I went for my first 5K run since the operation, and it felt so good. Exercising — especially running or cardio — helped me tackle the tiredness after radiotherapy.

I noticed slight redness of the radiated area of the breast. I felt quite tired until the end of the year. I even felt very dizzy on Christmas Day, like my iron levels had dropped — but they hadn't this time.

When I finished radiotherapy, it was coming up to a year since I first noticed the lumps. I was told that I would be closely monitored for about five years, with a mammogram of my left breast every year. I would also be shown how to self-check my right breast.

Because I hadn't heard anything, I called the specialist nurses and left a message. They referred me to a different team of specialist nurses, so I called them and left another message. When they rang me back, they said it would be best to talk about it at my next appointment with the plastic surgeon and their specialist nurses on 5th January. They also said that the mammogram is usually scheduled a year after surgery.

I questioned that, because the last time I had a mammogram of my left breast was in February 2023 — so I expected it to happen again in February 2024. But I was told that if I was concerned, I could bring it up at my appointment with the plastic surgeon and the nurses.

I felt like I was running around in circles.

I brought the topic up again when I received a call from a radiology specialist nurse, and this nurse confirmed to me that it should be a year from the last mammogram. She requested a mammogram for me in February.

I asked about the right breast, and said that self-checks don't offer me much reassurance. When I self-checked before the diagnosis and found lumps, it was already quite late and the cancer was spreading fast. She said that similarly, any imaging wouldn't necessarily catch it much earlier anyway.

This is one of the things that blows my mind. On one hand, you hear all about cancer prevention — self-checks, imaging, and the need for early detection. And that cancer survivors are monitored closely. On the other hand, once I completed treatment, I was told that the only monitoring I'd receive was a mammogram of my left breast once a year. And that this is because there isn't enough evidence that frequent scans reduce the risk of recurrence.

Which might be true. But doesn't early detection reduce mortality and the severity of treatment? For me, it probably would have made a big difference if I had found the lumps just a few months earlier. Maybe I could have had only a lumpectomy instead of a mastectomy. But I was also told that if the tumour had been too small, the mammogram wouldn't have detected it anyway. So actually, the so-called "close monitoring" is very limited and doesn't provide much reassurance.

I was told that if I wanted more frequent scans, I would need to get them done privately. I was told to do self-checks — but what does that even mean? How am I supposed to know? Especially with a reconstructed breast — how do I know what's normal?

IX

2024: The Year of Transition

2024 was a year of transition. It was about adjusting to a new "normal" — for me, in every area of life: personal, work, health, body changes, and a huge personal transformation.

I was in complete remission, having been told I was free from cancer on 26th September 2023. But things didn't end there — recovery, radiotherapy preparation, and treatment continued. It took me over a month to recover from radiotherapy, but as I mentioned before, it wasn't anything too disturbing. I just slept deeper and longer.

I had also been taking Ginkgo Biloba before, during, and after treatment, and I exercised regularly, which I felt helped me. But then, suddenly, after a few post-radiotherapy follow-up calls, I was discharged from main care. I was given a contact number to call if I had any concerns, but suddenly, it all felt very lonely. The whole of 2023 had been so busy with appointments and doctors' phone calls — if I needed anything, it was expedited. And then all of that was suddenly gone. It felt lonely and scary.

I'd get a tickle anywhere in my body and the first thing that would spring to mind was: Oh no — is that cancer?

I was dreading the mammogram in February. What if?! I used to get the results on the day — now I have to wait up to three weeks. It all feels very unsettling. I've learned to cope with it somehow, but it is very challenging at times. And it still doesn't stop me from worrying.

I still had 14 rounds of Phesgo injections, every three weeks. They didn't affect me much overall, but they were always very painful — and actually got more and more painful as time went on. I developed a red, bruised area around the injection site (a very regular shape). They prescribed a steroid cream to apply before each treatment, and monitored my heart, which remained absolutely perfect with no changes. At least I could have these injections at the outreach centre in the village every three weeks, where I saw nurses I already knew. I had phone calls with the oncologist every few weeks, but even those faded away later in the year.

My left toenail finally fell off in February, and a new one had grown halfway in. My hair was no longer fine baby hair — it had strengthened significantly, regrowing much darker and thicker.

Although I had a little sign that my period might return in November 2023, I had my first proper period on 27th January. It seemed like it had come back, but it went away again later in the year, so I wasn't sure whether I was peri-menopausal anyway.

Max recovered very well and was finally released from the crate.

I chose to continue looking after my body — sticking

to the healthy diet I set at the beginning of the journey, eliminating toxins from my diet and environment, still taking some supplements, juicing a few times per week, exercising, and practicing emotional and mental healing and clearing techniques. I am always on the lookout for new ways of living in a healthier and happier mind, body, and spirit.

On reflection, I would never have thought that the most difficult part of the journey would be the part after being declared free of cancer. Once I felt like the oncologist said, "Off you go." Interestingly, I had been so strong the whole time, and then, when things eased off, I struggled the most — especially with the radiotherapy. I wanted to move forward in life and leave it all behind, and what got to me the most was knowing that I would have to go through another three weeks of radiotherapy, with potential side effects appearing weeks after the treatments. That's when I broke down completely. I had moments during the journey, but this was the biggest one.

And the whole cancer journey didn't end when I became cancer-free. That's what I had imagined when I started treatment — that one day I would be declared free of cancer, and there would be a clear cut between the before and the after. But that's not the case.

It's similar to the COVID pandemic. It came, it was very intense, then we learned to deal with the uncertainty. It got better, then worse, then better again — but there was never a clear end date when everything suddenly returned to how it was before. That moment never actually happened. It just blended into a whole new world.

And this is exactly how it was with cancer. In the same way we say "before the pandemic" and "after the pandemic," now there is this "before and after the cancer diagnosis"

Cancer survivors are blessed with two lives. There is your life before cancer, and your life after. I am here to tell you your second life is going to be so much better than the first.

Breast cancer survivor Hoda Kotb

But what has helped me:

I created plans to stay on the top of the game. I tracked every appointment or future scan they told me about. And it proved to be not just beneficial but absolutely essential not to let things slip. Otherwise I would have had a different operation thinking I had a condition I didn't have, I would have started taking tablets for 10 years I didn't need, and I would have had to do 3 weeks course of radiotherapy instead of one.

The amazing people I have in my life me who supported me throughout the way and believed in me and my journey.

Surround yourself with only people who are going to lift you higher.

Oprah

Lifestyle changes including juicing during the whole journey and after to recover that supercharged my body. Interestingly, my vitamin levels were higher during chemo than now.

The cravings for doing fun things whilst feeling better between each chemo sessions helped me to create a lot of fun memories even during the most difficult time in my life. And when I look back I feel like I have more good memories than the bad ones in my mind.

I realised that going away between the chemo and the operation was the best thing I could do to reset my mind, body, and heart after the shock and traumatic experience with chemotherapy. It rebalanced me and made me more at peace and resilient for the next phase.

All the mind body healing techniques that helped me to work with my mind, all the energy and spiritual healing modalities that helped me to heal emotionally and strengthen my spiritual awareness and connection.

Life is 10% what happens to us and
90% how we react to it.

CHARLES R. SWINDOLL

And although I don't want to go through this or a similar experience ever again, the breast cancer was the biggest gift of my life. During this time, I experienced a profound transformation on all levels – physical, emotional, mental, spiritual.

First and foremost, I learnt how to love myself more – I realised that I learned how to look after my body better, discovered a more nurturing diet that makes me feel better, learnt how to detox my body regularly, how to look after my body better with nourishing skincare products, protecting my skin against the sun, and became more sensitive and aware of how I feel in my body and stand up for myself and my health.

I was worried to lose the breast originally, but despite the mastectomy (although the immediate reconstruction helped the situation), I don't feel like anyone else. It was still me, I feel complete. And surprisingly, I love my body more than I did before, with all its imperfections and scars.

I realised how fragile my life is and that I want to enjoy my time with my family more whilst we all can spend time together.

I realised how much pressure I actually put on myself by being a perfectionist, being a hyper-achiever. A lot I created a lot of stress in my old job myself. So looking back, I have to admit that it wasn't the old world so much as me who decided to carry all the problems on my shoulders and push hard for changing even things that were outside of my control. And that I no longer wanted to do this to myself.

I noticed that I push too hard in life, I struggle to let go of control, and that is how I block the flow instead of allowing everything to unfold, and that my biggest challenge is to move from doing to being.

Although we launched the property business, did our first renovation project, and launched 2 short-term let properties, I was still holding off to the old life during the year 2024, trying to get some job security through contracting in product development, or even going back to my previous job with reduced hours, as well as looking for new income streams. It was a year of exploration of new avenues, building up my confidence and belief in myself in order to step into my life purpose. The Universe made me by closing all the doors into the past and beginning to open the new ones. It is scary and exciting at the same time.

I lost the Employee Tribunal and didn't get any compensation from the company that withdrew their offer. It was a deep hurt emotionally, as I didn't want them to get away with it. But they were able to show evidence that they were just a mess, not discriminators. But one thing is certain, if I started the job there, I would end up once again overworked, stressed, and unfulfilled.

I am not sure if it was Malta exactly, but it is by the sea where my soul belongs, and I am still waiting for this chapter to unfold. As I now believe that things have their time and place.

I understood some of the emotional and spiritual causes of the illness, like a deep grief, unresolved hurt, suppressed emotions, a traumatic shock, and blocked own defending power.

It also taught me that it is OK to ask for help and to be more aware of the need for the balance of giving and receiving in my life. And that I don't need to feel guilty for every help and support I receive, and that I don't have to pay it off immediately, to the same person in the same way. But maybe pay it forward, in a different way, to a different person, at a different time.

It helped me to find passion and purpose in wanting to help other people and also the confidence that I can do this. Otherwise, I would just think about how I could help others and doubt that I could even help others for the rest of my life.

The freedom to be who I truly am and let go of fear of judgement and worry of what others think. I learnt to do things out of love instead of fear. I discovered a deep sense of purpose that is the driving force to push through all the fear, doubts, and makes me more courageous.

Be who you are and say what you feel, because those who mind don't matter and those who matter don't mind

Dr. Seuss

This transformation helped me to feel emotionally and spiritually more connected to myself, the Universe, God, and the Angels. I no longer hang on to the words as I did before — it is my world, and also, they are just words, and they only have the meaning we give them. Because spirituality, for me, means being my true self and realising the Divine within — a deep connection to my soul and alignment with my soul's purpose. And to experience oneness, a feeling of deep, unconditional love for myself as well as for others.

It strengthened my connection to the Divine, and it proved

to my logical brain that the Silva Method and mind control techniques really work — as does Reiki.

To fulfil my dreams, and to pursue what I had put on my vision, but also to live life more fully — to be more spontaneous and let the Universe unfold things, rather than overplanning everything.

And eventually, I stepped fully into my life's purpose.

And here I am — a new version of me. A Breast Cancer Coach, Mentor, and Therapist, helping other women navigate breast cancer. Supporting them through the difficult journey, and helping to support their healing on all levels — physical, mental, emotional, and spiritual. Helping them — and other breast cancer survivors — to rebuild their new lives and identities beyond the breast cancer experience, with clarity and confidence. Just as I did for myself.

Many survivors experience the moment when the celebration of being clear of cancer is soon replaced by the "survivor's guilt." But I strongly believe that healing comes from the grace of God.

Not because one person deserves to overcome cancer more than another, or because someone is luckier than someone else. But because to survive means… it wasn't the right time to transition to the other side yet.

And there is a mission on this planet to be accomplished first…

And another lesson to be learnt…

And another story to be written…

And another chance to live a life true to ourselves…

And another opportunity to make this world a better place to live in…

Because life is a gift we've been given; what we do with it, and how we share it, is our gift in return.

The freedom to be yourself is a gift only you can give yourself. But once you do, no one can take it away.

DOE ZANTAMATA

X

Claim Your Free Bonuses – Just For You!

If you want to learn the tools and techniques I used for this profound transformation, I've created some beautiful resources to support you as you continue your transformation journey.

Visit www.lotus-journey.com/book-bonuses
to access:

- Free Healing Meditation Download
- Templates & Tools to support your vision, mindset, and wellness
- Exclusive Discounts on my services as well as on products I use and recommend
- Additional Support Resources to help you thrive

All you need to do is sign up, and everything will be delivered straight to your inbox.

XI
Let's Stay Connected

Thank you from the bottom of my heart for joining me on this journey. Whether you're a breast cancer warrior, a seeker on the path of healing, survivor, or someone looking to live a more purposeful life, your story matters. And I want to hear it.

Share your story with me

I believe in the power of storytelling. If my journey has inspired you, I invite you to share your own. Send me a message, join the community, or tag me on social media—I'd be honoured to hear from you.

I'd love to know how this book has impacted you. Whether it sparked a shift, brought comfort, or raised new questions, your voice is important.

www.lotus-journey.com/book-feedback

Stay in touch

Join my online community and follow me here:
Website (Breast Cancer Support): www.lotus-journey.com
Website (Personal Brand): www.veronika-bubenickova.com

Social Media:
Facebook: facebook.com/lotusjourneycom
Instagram: @veronika_bubenickova
YouTube: @lotus-journey-com
LinkedIn: linkedin.com/in/veronika-bubenickova

Together, we heal. Together, we rise.

With love,

Veronika x
Your spark in the dark

XII
Glossary

Chemo(therapy) Cycle — A period of chemotherapy treatment followed by a rest period. A full chemotherapy plan is typically divided into multiple cycles to allow the body time to recover between treatments.

Chemo(therapy) Treatment — A cancer treatment that uses drugs to destroy cancer cells, typically by stopping their ability to grow and divide and that can be administered either at the hospital directly into veins or in a form of pills at home.

DIEP Flap — A type of breast reconstruction surgery that uses skin and fat from the lower abdomen (but not muscle) to rebuild the breast after mastectomy.

ECG (Electrocardiogram) — A medical test that records the electrical activity of the heart over a period of time using electrodes placed on the skin.

Grade — In cancer, grade refers to how much cancer cells look like healthy cells under a microscope. A lower grade means the cancer cells look more normal and are usually slower growing.

HER2 Positive — A type of breast cancer that tests positive for a protein called human epidermal growth factor receptor 2 (HER2), which promotes cancer cell growth. HER2-positive cancers tend to grow and spread faster but often respond well to targeted therapies.

Lumpectomy — A breast-conserving surgery in which only the tumour and a small margin of surrounding tissue are removed, rather than the whole breast.

Mammogram — An X-ray image of the breast used to detect and diagnose breast diseases, especially breast cancer.

Mastectomy — Surgery to remove all or part of the breast, typically to treat or prevent breast cancer.

Mother Meera — A spiritual teacher believed by followers to be an embodiment of the Divine Mother, known for her silent *darshan* (blessing) and work on spiritual consciousness.

NHS — The publicly funded healthcare system in the United Kingdom.

Phesgo — A combination of two targeted therapy drugs, Herceptin (trastuzumab) and Perjeta (pertuzumab), used to treat HER2-positive breast cancer.

Programming — In this context, likely refers to mental or subconscious programming and how beliefs and patterns are formed in the mind. Also associated with personal development methods.

Sai Baba — A spiritual master from India, known for his teachings on love, service, and the unity of all religions. There are two well-known spiritual figures known as Sai Baba: Shirdi Sai Baba and Sathya Sai Baba.

Sai Centre — A spiritual gathering place or community group dedicated to the teachings of Sai Baba, where devotional singing, service activities, and study sessions are held.

Silva Method — A self-help and meditation program developed by José Silva that focuses on improving the mind's ability to heal, solve problems, and achieve goals through altered states of consciousness.

Sentinel Lymph Node Biopsy — A surgical procedure used to determine whether breast cancer has spread to the lymph nodes. The sentinel nodes are the first few lymph nodes into which a tumour drains.

Targeted Therapy — A type of cancer treatment that targets specific genes or proteins involved in the growth and survival of cancer cells. It's often used for HER2-positive breast cancer.

Toastmasters — A global organisation that helps people improve their public speaking and leadership skills through structured meetings and practice sessions.

Trello Board — An online project management tool that uses boards, lists, and cards to help organise tasks, ideas, and projects, often used for personal planning or team collaboration.

www.ingramcontent.com/pod-product-compliance
Ingram Content Group UK Ltd.
Pitfield, Milton Keynes, MK11 3LW, UK
UKHW042148160725
460867UK00001BA/1